GREENWOOD
GUIDES

THE GREENWOOD GUIDE TO
NEW ZEALAND

Sixth Edition

hand-picked accommodation

www.greenwoodguides.com

Series Editor **Simon Greenwood**
Writing collaboration and inspections **Joe Wallace** and **Simon Greenwood**
Maps © Collins Bartholomew Ltd 2009.
Reproduced by permission of HarperCollins www.collinsbartholomew.com.
Design and layout **Tory Gordon-Harris**
Printing, **Colorcraft**, Hong Kong
UK Distribution, **Portfolio**, London
NZ Distribution, **Addenda Publishing Ltd.**, Auckland

The cover image is of **Brancott Ridge**, entry number 55, by Frank Gasteiger
Title page image: **Blue Duck Lodge** entry number 37
North Island intro page image: **Magic Cottage** entry number 5
South Island intro page image: **Cove Cottage** entry number 53

First published in 2001 by Greenwood Guides,
12 Avalon Rd, London SW6 2EX, UK.

Sixth edition

Copyright © September 2009 Greenwood Guides

All rights reserved. No part of this publication may be reproduced, or transmitted
in any form or by any means, electronically or mechanically, including photocopying,
recording or any information storage or retrieval system without prior written
permission from the publisher. This publication is not included under licences issued
by the Copyright Agency. No part of this publication may be used in any form of
advertising, sales promotion or publicity.

Simon Greenwood has asserted his right to be identified as the author of this work.

ISBN 978-0-9551160-7-0

Printed in China through Colorcraft Ltd., Hong Kong.

Simon Greenwood

Joe Wallace

CONTENTS

Introduction
Maps
Symbols and what they mean
Distances chart

NORTH ISLAND

SOUTH ISLAND

introduction

Whatever you think of the look of this guide (and we hope that you like it, of course) we know that in the end we will not be judged by the book's cover but by its content. In other words we need to be a major reason why you enjoyed your holiday.

To this end we are particularly fussy about whom we accept into the guide, relying only on our own experience. I hope this will become apparent to first-time users of the guide once you hit the road.

New Zealand and The Greenwood Guide to Hand-picked Accommodation

The Creator seems to have had a soft spot for New Zealand. It doesn't matter where in the country you go. All His (or Her) state-of-the-art, top-of-the-range showpiece scenery items are on display: bays sprinkled with islands, snow-capped volcanoes, bright blue mountain lakes, sea cliffs and rocky coves, rivers and waterfalls in semi-tropical rainforest, white-sand beaches, ancient and giant trees, green grassy hills that suddenly plummet into river gorges. And so it goes on. The landscape is relentlessly awe-inspiring.

And yet the place isn't crawling with tourists like you'd think it would be. It's too far away for most Europeans. If these islands were found in the Mediterranean, you can be sure they would not be the Utopian travel destination that they are today. If you want to share some of the world's most varied and beautiful scenery with just a handful of film crews... and at the same time enjoy highly sophisticated levels of comfort and hospitality... AND, most vitally of all, be looked after by genuinely friendly, well-travelled, humorous, down-to-earth hosts, then you're going to have to travel further than most people can be bothered. New Zealand's remoteness is precisely what keeps it precious.

It's simplicity itself to hire a car and drive around under your own steam. All you really need is someone to tell you the most exciting and friendly places to stay. Enter triumphantly the Greenwood Guide to New Zealand....

This is now the sixth edition so we are really pretty clued up about places to stay in New Zealand. We have made several hundred visits over the years and have whittled down the final entries to just 86, evenly spread across both islands.

We have found extraordinary places to stay at all levels of the price spectrum, except the extravagantly expensive (which you can certainly find in NZ) and the suspiciously cheap. Great accommodation is not defined by how much you pay and what you get for your money. It is a complex compound of atmosphere, location, creature comfort and human interaction. We gravitate towards places that have something I'm going to call 'soul', like it or not.

Our natural biases often lean towards the lived-in feel, artistic inclination, creative design, historical interest... but only if these qualities are backed up by owners who have a real liking for other people and take a real pleasure in looking after them. Only the character and humanity of each place determine its acceptability.

At its simplest the Greenwood Guides approach is to recommend places that we have been to ourselves and particularly liked.

This is not a full-blown directory of accommodation therefore. You will often be disappointed if you expect to find a Greenwood place in a particular town. Not every town has great places to stay. The book is designed to be followed as a guide book. Stay in our places as destinations in themselves and meet lovely, warm, friendly, humorous New Zealanders.

This is not just for self-propelling overseas travellers looking for something a bit magical and different from their holiday. Kiwis will love these places just as much.

Expensive does not Mean Good

There are essentially three types of place to stay. There are those that fulfil their obligations in a commercial way and leave you feeling throughout your stay like the paying customer that you are. And there are those few great places where you are welcomed in and treated as a friend, cliché though this may now have become, and where paying at the end of your visit is a pleasurable surprise. And, of course, there are those places where paying is a disagreeable inevitability!

It is a particular irony of the accommodation world that no price is ever put on the essential qualities of a place – people, atmosphere, charm. These terms are too woolly, perhaps, to quantify, but this is where one's real enjoyment of a place to stay stems from. You are asked to pay instead for tangible facilities like marble bathrooms and en-suite showers.

This is a fallacy that we try to dismantle in all our guides, which is why you will find places at all reasonable price levels. Expensive does not mean good. And nor does cheap, however appealing the word may sound! If a place costs plenty then it will probably offer facilities in keeping with the price. But that does not mean that you will have any fun. Some very expensive places forget that they are providing a service and look down their noses at their own guests. At the other end of the scale, the very cheapest places are often cheap for good reasons. Sometimes for spectacular reasons!

Character and genuine hospitality, the extra qualities we search for, are found spaced evenly across the price spectrum. Nowhere in this guide cuts corners at the risk of your displeasure. We give equal billing to each place we choose, no matter if it is a gorgeous lodge or a home-spun B&B.

At the top end, the most jewel-encrusted, nay 'boutique' places may drip with luxurious trimmings, but have retained their sense of atmosphere and humour, are friendly and informal and are still owned and managed by the same people.

Equally, there are places in the book that do not have much in the way of luxury, but easily compensate with unique settings, wonderful views and charming hosts.

It is the quality of experience that draws us in and this is not determined by how much you pay. In the end I know that you will really like the owners in this book, many of whom we now count as friends. And you will certainly make friends yourselves if you stick to the Greenwood trail.

Driving

One point worth making is that, although this is not the largest country in the world, you can easily underestimate how long it takes to get from A to B (and on to C). This is because: a) many NZ roads twist and wind their way around hills, volcanoes and other mountainous terrain and there's not much anyone can do about that; b) there is a culture of slow driving in NZ, a practice encouraged by conscientious traffic cops; and c) it seems impossible to overtake anyone, despite the small number of cars on the roads. So I recommend you leave lots of time to get where you're going, relax into it and enjoy the impossibly lovely scenery that seems to line every road in the country.

Car Hire in New Zealand

The best way to see New Zealand is by car. Most of our epic research period in New Zealand was spent behind the wheel of one of About New Zealand's rental cars. We always found them helpful, friendly and great value. They also have bases throughout the country, which is always handy when travelling from point A to point B. About New Zealand Head Office: 33 Iversen Terrace, Christchurch, freephone: 0800-45-55-65, phone: +64 3 3666 094, fax: +64 3 3666 069, email: aboutnz@rentalcar.co.nz.

It is a good idea to book your car hire and accommodation in advance. In peak season both can get booked up very quickly.

Inter-island Ferries

You can fly or ferry between the two islands; both methods are scenic treats. From Picton, Bluebridge and Interlander Ferries take their cargo of cars and passengers out into the Cook Strait, a bright strip of dolphin-filled sea, fringed by the intermittent islands and lush hilly fingers of The Marlborough Sounds. You'll be received at the other end by winking lights and the lively sweeping embrace of Wellington Harbour.
Bluebridge Cook Strait Ferry www.bluebridge.co.nz 04-471-6188.
Interislander Ferry www.interislander.co.nz 04-498-3302.

Directions

We have provided directions, unless a 30-word spiel was unlikely to clarify matters, i.e. if a place is in the middle of a town or city. Most owners can fax detailed maps/directions or they will have a web site that can help.

Pay for Entry

We could not afford to research and publish this guide in the way we do without the financial support of those we feature. Each place to stay that we have chosen has paid an entry fee for which we make no apology. It has not influenced our decision-making about who is right or wrong for the guide and we turn down many more than we accept. The proof of this is in the proverbial pudding. Use the book and see for yourself. It is also very hard for us to write up a place that we are not enthusiastic about.

Prices and Payment

Prices are quoted in New Zealand dollars per couple sharing per night, unless specifically stated otherwise. Single rates are also given. We have provided a range to allow for expected price increases over two years. There might be unexpected increases if the property changes radically or exchange rates alter, in which case we would ask you to be understanding.

Quite a few places do not accept payment with credit cards – these have a symbol in the book – but may take travellers' cheques or other forms of payment. Again, ask when booking.

Maps

The maps in this book are not road maps, but merely general indicators of where the properties are. You should get a detailed road map when you arrive.

Cancellation

Cancellation policies vary as much as the wallpaper and should be clarified on booking. Many establishments will ask for a credit card number when you book so that they are not wholly compromised if you fail to turn up.

Smoking

It is most unlikely that anyone will want you to smoke indoors.

Telephones

Calling New Zealand from abroad: the international dialling code is 64. So to call New Zealand from Britain, you key 00 64, then the eight-digit phone number.

Disclaimer

We make no claims to god-like objectivity in assessing what is or is not special about the places we feature. They are there because we like them. Our opinions and tastes are mortal and ours alone. We have done our utmost to get the facts right, but apologise for any mistakes that may have slipped through the net. Some things change which are outside our control: people sell up, prices increase, exchange rates fluctuate, unfortunate extensions are added, marriages break up and even acts of God can rain down destruction. We would be grateful to be told about any errors or changes, however great or small. We can always make these edits on the web version of this book.

Please write to us

My email address is **simon@greenwoodguides.com** for all comments. We are always grateful to hear how much/little you enjoyed the places in the book.

We also have a guide to South African Accommodation (with Namibia) and you can also find Australian and Canadian accommodation online at **www.greenwoodguides.com.**

Finally a huge thank-you to Joe Wallace. He took on the challenge of researching and inspecting the entire book himself and drove tirelessly all over New Zealand during the four-month research period. You are the happy inheritor of the fruits of his efforts. I am sure you will enjoy your trip.

Simon.

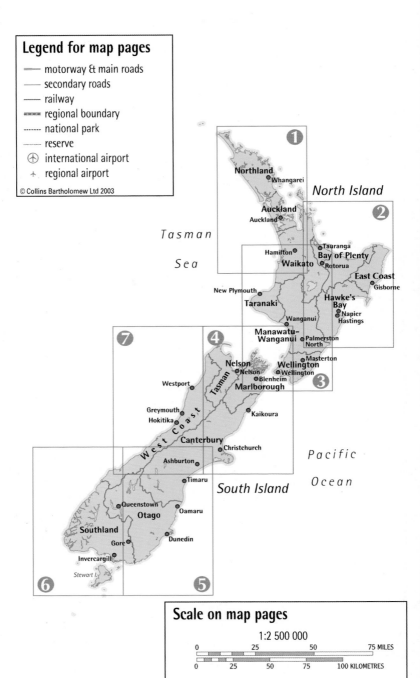

Legend for map pages

— motorway & main roads
— secondary roads
— railway
━━━ regional boundary
------ national park
.... reserve
⊕ international airport
✈ regional airport

© Collins Bartholomew Ltd 2003

①

Northland
● Whangarei

North Island

②

Auckland
● Auckland

Tasman

Sea

Hamilton ●
● Tauranga
Bay of Plenty
Waikato
● Rotorua

East Coast
● Gisborne

New Plymouth ●
Taranaki
Hawke's
Bay
Wanganui ●
● Napier
● Hastings

Manawatu-
Wanganui
● Palmerston
North

⑦

④

● Masterton
Nelson
Wellington
● Nelson
● Wellington
● Blenheim
Marlborough
③

Westport ●

Tasman

Greymouth ●
Hokitika ●
● Kaikoura

West Coast

Canterbury
● Christchurch

Ashburton ●

Pacific

● Timaru
South Island

Ocean

Queenstown ●
Otago
● Oamaru

Southland
Gore ●
● Dunedin

Invercargill ●

Stewart I.

⑥

⑤

Scale on map pages

1:2 500 000

0   25   50   75 MILES

0   25   50   75   100 KILOMETRES

Accommodation entry numbers are flagged in red.

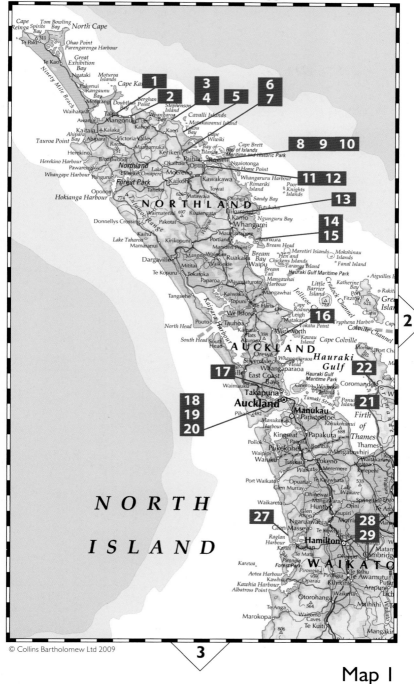

Map 1

© Collins Bartholomew Ltd 2009

Map 2

© Collins Bartholomew Ltd 2009

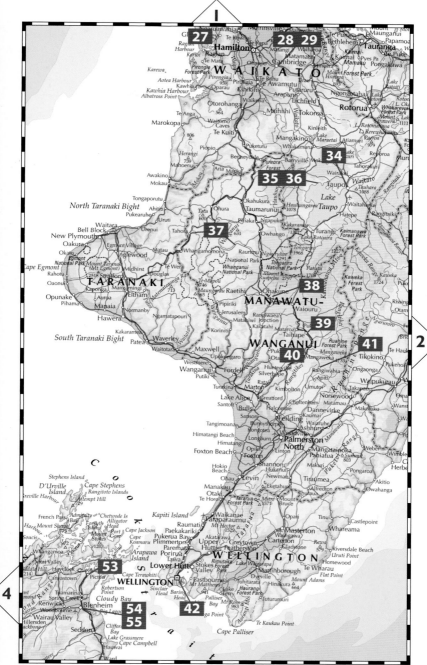

Map 3

© Collins Bartholomew Ltd 2009

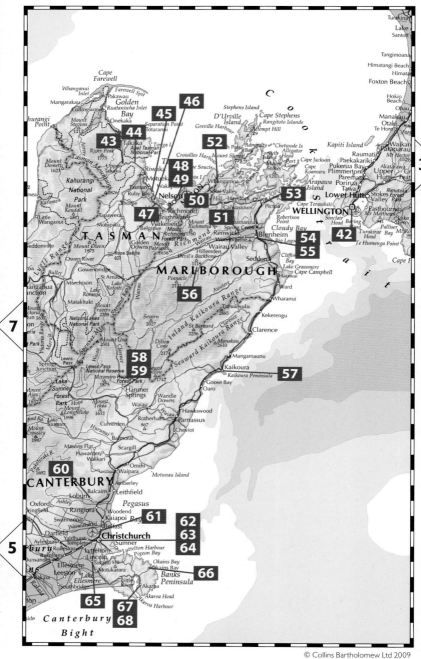

Map 4

© Collins Bartholomew Ltd 2009

SOUTH ISLAND

Map 5

© Collins Bartholomew Ltd 2009

Map 6

© Collins Bartholomew Ltd 2009

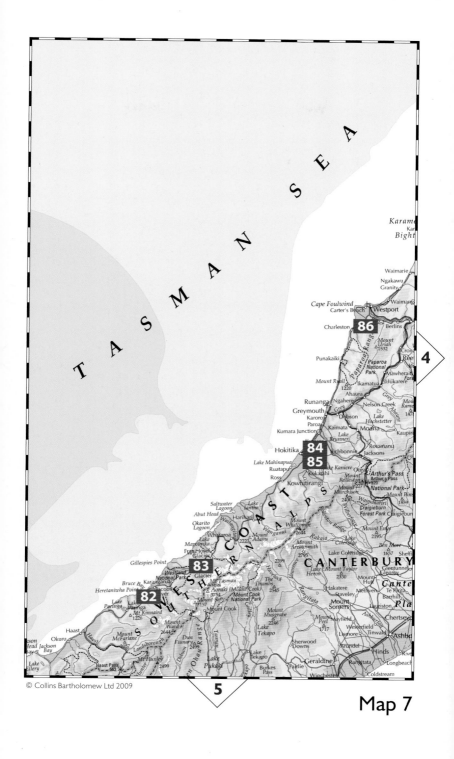

T A S M A N   S E A

Karame
Kara
Bight

Waimarie
Ngakawu
Granity
Cape Foulwind
Carter's Beach ·Westport·
Charleston **86** · Berlins
Mount Uriah 1532 ·Cron
Rēe
Punakaiki
Paparoa National Park ·Mawherai
Mount Rväll 1220 Ikamatua ·Hukarere
Ahaura
Runanga Ngahere Nelson Creek
Greymouth Karoro Dobson Lake Hochstetter *Mou* *Rame* 1421
Paroa
Kumara Junction Kaimata Moana
Lake Brunner Kaupir
Hokitika **84** Rotomanu
85 Kokiri Jacksons
Lake Mahinapua Lake Kaniere
Ruatapu *Mount Rolleston* Arthur's Pass
Ross Arthur's Pass National Park
Kowhitirangi *Mount* *Murchison* *Mount Rin*
Saltwater *Lagoon* Lake Ianthe Forest Park Craigieour
Abut Head Harihari
Okarito Lagoon *Mount Eno* 2195
Whataroa *Mount* *Whitcombe* *Rakaia*
Franz Josef Glacier *Mount* *Adams* *Mount* *Arrowsmith* Ben Mor
Gillespies Point *Mount* *Coleridge*
Westland National Park **83** Glacier *Hakatere*
Bruce B *Mt Tasman* 3498 *Aoraki/Mount Cook* *Mount* *Somers*
Heretaniwha Point Jacobs *Mount Sefton National Park* Staveley
Lake *Paringa* **82** *Mt Kinnaird* 1226 Mount Cook *Mount* *Peel* Lauriston
Okuru *Mount* *McFarlane* 2057 *Mount* *Musgrave* Mayfield
Head Jackson *Mt Huxley* 2399 Sherwood Ashbu
Bay Lake Tekapo Downs
Lake Ellery Haast Pass 563 *Lake* *Pukaki* Geraldine Hinds
Burkes Pass Fairlie
Lake Tekapo Winchester Coldstream

S O U T H E R N   A L P S

WEST COAST

CANTERBURY

Cante
Pla

© Collins Bartholomew Ltd 2009

4

5

Map 7

SYMBOLS

and What They Mean

 No credit cards accepted

 There is a restaurant on the premises or meals can be provided

 Rooms all have TV

 Children are welcome without conditions

 Wireless Internet access

 Working farm

 Off-street car parking

 Full wheelchair facilities

 Access only for wheelchairs

 Swimming available in pool, sea or river

 No smoking anywhere inside the buildings

 Good walking from the house

 Fishing organised here

 Horse-riding available here

Distances chart

The maximum speed limit on New Zealand's roads is 100km/hr. Due to its hilly and mountainous terrain, average speeds are lower and it always takes slightly longer than expected to arrive at your destination. All the more reason to relax into your drive and really enjoy the spectacular scenery out of the window.

Distances in kilometres

NORTH ISLAND

km	Gisborne	Hamilton	Kaitaia	Napier	N. Plym	Paihia	Rotorua	Taupo	Tauranga	Waitomo	Wangonui	Well'ton
Auckland	449	127	325	423	357	241	234	280	206	202	457	658
Gisborne		394	823	216	585	739	287	332	298	445	468	538
Hamilton			452	296	231	368	107	153	107	75	331	532
Kaitaia				748	681	108	558	602	531	524	779	983
Napier					412	661	225	143	299	307	252	323
N. Plym						597	299	296	308	173	160	355
Paihia							474	518	445	440	697	898
Rotorua								80	86	166	309	460
Taupo									156	163	229	380
Tauranga										151	439	545
Waitomo											273	439
Wangonui												195

SOUTH ISLAND

km	Christ'ch	Dunedin	Fr Josef	Grey'th	Inv'gill	M. Cook	Nelson	Picton	Q'town	Te Anau	Wanaka	Westport
Blenheim	321	683	520	331	899	651	117	29	808	971	749	265
Christ'ch		361	408	255	578	330	417	350	487	650	428	336
Dunedin			570	565	217	319	799	711	281	289	276	670
Fr Josef				189	542	506	485	549	365	539	294	294
Grey'th					731	524	296	360	554	728	483	105
Inv'gill						445	1016	928	189	159	248	836
M. Cook							747	680	271	426	212	629
Nelson								113	850	1024	779	230
Picton									837	1000	778	294
Q'town										166	71	659
Te Anau											245	823
Wanaka												588

North Island

North Island - Northland

Macrocarpa Cottage

Jamie and Sara Rogers
2 Bush Point Road, Taipa, Mangonui
Tel: 09-406-1245
Email: maccotage@xtra.co.nz Web: www.holidayhouses.co.nz/properties/1515.asp

The best place to laze around inside is on the window-seat in the corner - you can watch the fish swim by below. Macrocarpa is heavenly. Jamie built it from scratch and the deck hangs out over the Taipa River as it turns left past the sand spit and spills into Doubtless Bay. The view stretches up to Tokerau beach on the Karikari Peninsula about ten kilometres away and a wall of glass in the downstairs bedroom means you don't have to get out of bed for it. If you do make it to a vertical position, roll ten metres down to the shore and swim in crystal clear water when the tide is in. The cottage is spic and span, simply furnished and flooded with light. It's all open-plan, with a good queen-size bed, a sitting area, a kitchen downstairs and a twin-bedded room in the loft. Jamie and Sara are young, mellow and know all the best spots in the area, including deserted beaches of silica sand – probably the best in New Zealand - and mangrove swamps. Jamie not only managed to talk to me, but he also got dinner ready for his in-laws and entertained his children, all at the same time and with no apparent effort. This relaxed attitude has spread to the cottage and I challenge you not to feel supremely zoned-out by the time you leave.

Rooms: 1 cottage with 1 double and 1 twin sharing a shower room.
Price: $120 - $150. Extra adults $20, kids $10.
Meals: Self-catering.
Directions: West through Cable Bay on SH10. Up hill to Taipa, then down hill with estuary on right. Cottage on right and signed, but turning impossible, so pass and do a U-turn.

Entry Number: 1

Beach Lodge

Margaret Morrison
121 State Highway 10, Coopers Beach, Mangonui Far North
Tel: 09-406-0068 Fax: 09-406-0068
Email: margaret@beachlodge.co.nz Web: www.beachlodge.co.nz

One of Margaret's guests, an ambassador to New Zealand, was overjoyed to have found 'paradise' here at Beach Lodge. This is not faint praise considering that he was sent from Brazil. Approaching in my car it took only a fleeting glimpse to see exactly what he meant. Fringed by the crimson trail of blossoming pohutukawa trees, with soft waves gently licking the shore, the lodge presides over the most exquisitely golden and deserted sands I had come across in NZ. Set just above the trees each apartment has a large deck from which to gaze to the shore and you are just a few steps away from making the beach your own. In true pioneering spirit, Margaret returned from her travels some years ago to find her plot and build her bach. Bright and open-plan with high ceilings and big french windows that encourage the sea breeze in and swirl it around, the apartments are places for easy holiday living. One minute you'll be on the kitchen bar stools dangling your legs and eating lunch and the next you'll have jumped back in your kayak and be paddling offshore. I loved the recent addition with its rustic whitewashed finishes and kaleidoscope of bathroom mirrors for those 'are there really seven of me or did I have one too many gins at sundown?' moments. Best of all is Margaret herself, a spirited lady and a no-nonsense bon viveur. She knows all the special spots in this largely - and thankfully - undiscovered part of the North Island. Golf, boats and personalised trips to Cape Reinga can be organised from here. *Wifi broadband.*

Rooms: 5 self-contained apartments: 4 with 1 queen and 1 twin and a shared shower; 1 with 1 queen and en-suite shower.
Price: $195 - $450 per lodge per night.
Meals: Fully self-catering.
Directions: From Auckland take SH1 north to Whangarei. Continue along SH1 to Kawakawa, then turn L keeping on same highway. Turn R onto SH 10 towards Bay of Islands and Doubtless Bay. Go past turn-off to Mangonui. Beach Lodge is on beachfront 1km from the Coopers Beach sign and 60km sign.

Crab Cove

Dave Crabb
Mahinepua Rd, Mahinepua Peninsula
Tel: 09-405-0075 Fax: 09-405-1176
Email: crabcove@xtra.co.nz Web: www.waterfrontretreat.co.nz
Cell: 021-804-889

Dave has created this cave-cottage mainly, I think, because he wanted to see the look on your face when you arrive. The cottage is literally woven into the hillside, the roof covered with grass. The 'cave mouth' opens onto a deck where two chairs have been placed as if with tweezers. Another few yards and you'd be plummeting down the cliff to your own rocky cove below. There is a path that descends more gently, if more slowly. The cove, leaned over by old pohutukawa trees clutching the cliff-face with talon-like roots, has kayaks for exploring the nearby sea-caves. Or one of Dave's great pleasures is to take guests out diving or crayfish-hunting. Dave's many hats of expertise include that of master-builder/architect...but he was also no less than NZ skateboard champion. If a thing's worth doing....The cottage is a single open-plan room with a low bed looking straight out to sea. There is a blue-glass shower behind the scenes and a sauna. Small bottles of champagne sit in the fridge alongside the excellent breakfast provisions. If you can book Crab Cove stay as long as you can. No wife/husband/partner will be able to repay you elsewhere without spending their life savings. Simple yet sensational. (The instinct to call it The Crabb Cave of Crab Cove must have been hard to resist!)

Rooms: 1 cottage with king, en-suite shower and sauna.
Price: $350.
Meals: Breakfast basket provided.
Directions: From Kerikeri 40 mins. 18.8km north of Keri' turn R, Matauri Bay. After 14.4km L signed Te Ngaere Bay – follow for 7km. R at Mahinepua Rd, over bridge and then immediately L. Electric gates, ask for code when booking. 300m turn R past Private Property sign.

Map Number: 1

Entry Number: 3

Huntaway Lodge

Diane and David Lennan

1692 Wainui Rd, Te Ngaere Bay, Kaeo
Tel: 09-405-1611 Fax: 09-405-1612
Email: info@huntawaylodgenz.com Web: www.huntawaylodgenz.com

Huntaway Lodge is small (just five rooms) and superb, perched on a hillside with a wide balcony deck overlooking three pristine wine-glass bays and the ocean and Cavalli Islands beyond. Modern comforts in the lodge and retreat are in plentiful supply: wonderful bathrooms, heated floors, hidden TVs/DVDs/CDs and a companion library of specially-selected films and music. There are as many extras as you can think up without being ridiculous: chocolates and port in the bedrooms, boogie boards, kayaks, towels for the beach and a superb spa pool with infinity ocean views to die for; just the place for a sunset drink and dreams. All the rooms open onto private areas of the deck where you will linger under parasols with a bottle of wine before dinner... or perhaps all day. Dinner can be taken al fresco and food is specially prepared to suit tastes and dietary requirements by the wonderful resident chef. The central guest area is an open contemporary space with comfy sofas, fresh flowers, modern art, games to play and places to relax. The gardens have been designed and planted to give guests a real NZ experience. The aim is to allow you the feeling that this is your private house, but to provide excellent personal service and 'tailored' dining with it.

Rooms: 5: 3 queens, 2 kings all with en-suite shower.
Price: $495 - $695. Room rates only.
Meals: Full breakfast incl. Dinners $90 p.p. (3 courses and pre-dinner nibbles). There is a wine list. Picnics available. Late arrival options.
Directions: SH10 from Kerikeri north for 18.8km to Matauri Bay Tourist Rte. R here, 14.4km, L at Matauri Bay intersection. Follow Wainui Rd 5km, thro' Te Ngaere Bay, 600m after 100 kmph sign turn L thro' gates behind Huntaway Lodge sign.

Magic Cottages at Takou River

Anna and Ian Sizer

660 Takou Bay Road, Kerikeri
Tel: 09-407-8065
Email: takouriver@xtra.co.nz Web: www.takouriver.com
Cell: 027-545-7633

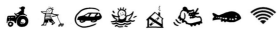

When I visited, Takou was shrouded in mist, but the story-book scenery of the valley still revealed itself in tantalising glimpses, particularly along the river; silver fog sheeting over rolling hills, native birds swooping between branches of contorted river trees, a broad river sweeping along the property's border and out to the pristine sands of Takou Bay Beach. Here nature is at its most seductive, even at night when you can hear the rare call of kiwis from your bedroom. There are kayaks and fishing-rods, so no excuses; paddle the river to the coast, stopping off at one of the swimming holes to catch kowhai, mullet or snapper for dinner (you're in self-catered cottages after all). The environmentally-aware Sizers (the farm is certified organic) have planted 10,000 native trees and the sub-tropical gardens around the very private cottages provide seclusion as well as natural comfort with their salvaged native timber floors and, on the decks of River and Summer Cottages, alfresco claw-foot baths. The lodge is ideal for a group of four, especially during winter with its schist wood-burner and spa bath, while solar-powered Magic Cottage, idyllically placed beside the pohutukawa-lined river, with its romantic alfresco clawfoot bath on the deck will thrill honeymooners. There's a pretty extensive wine trail up here in Northland and the famous Kauri Cliffs golf course is 25 minutes away, so day trips away from Takou are not much trouble; but then they're not that necessary either. This place will remind you what life is all about.

Rooms: Magic Cottage 1 superking, en/s & alfresco bath; The Lodge 1 superking en/s spa bath; 1 king/twin bath & sh'r; River Cottage 1 king/tw en/s bath & 1 queen en/s sh'r & alfresco bath; Summer Cottage 1 king/tw en/s bath & 1 qu en/s bath & alfr' bath.
Price: 2 people $190 - $250 per night; 3/4 people $300 - $350 per night.
Meals: Fully self-catered, so bring own provisions.
Directions: Don't drive into Kerikeri, carry straight on up SH10 from Waipapa. Drive about 8km north then take a right on Takou Bay Road. Drive on, turn left as the road forks and Takou River is at the very end. Full directions provided when booking.

Map Number: 1

Entry Number: 5

Stone Store Lodge

Richard Miller

201 Kerikeri Road, Kerikeri
Tel: 09-407-6693 Fax: 09-407-6693
Email: richard@stonestorelodge.co.nz Web: www.stonestorelodge.co.nz
Cell: 027-233-0602

Though many guesthouses like to promote themselves as 'a home away from home', very few actually are. And so it was with no little delight that while rootling around in Kerikeri for GG gems, I unearthed Stone Store Lodge, a clear exception to the rule. Clearly not a man to shy away from a challenge, Richard sold his farm to spend a couple of years sailing the high seas in the South Pacific, and then when the time was right, he returned to shore, trading water for a patch of land on which to build himself a lodge. And here it is, teetering on the hillside behind town looking out over sub-tropical native bush to Kerikeri's famed historic Stone Store by the watery inlet below. Glimpses of Richard's former life are framed on the walls in daughter Lucy's fantastic photographs, an exotic mix of colour and cultures and endless points of conversation. Purposefully designed for privacy and utmost comfort, the rooms, like the rest of the house, are beautifully presented and elegantly ethno-chic, with huge walk-in showers, flowers by the bed, floor-to-ceiling windows to soak up the early morning sunshine and a private outdoor bath for starry nights. You'll have the run of the house with its many spots inside and out to sit and linger and there's even an old piano in the corner. This is a happy place that makes packing to leave a dire business performed with reluctant step and a heavy heart!

Rooms: 3: all kings with en-suite showers.
Price: $175 - $230.
Meals: Full breakfast included. Home wood-fired pizzas for dinner by prior arrangement $30 pp for four guests or more. Good Restaurants within walking distance.
Directions: From SH10, turn into Kerikeri. Follow signs to St James's Church and the Historic Stone Store, the lodge is just before these, sign-posted on the right.

Bed of Roses

Louisa and Cliff Hobson-Corry

165 Kerikeri Road, Kerikeri
Tel: 09-407-4666
Email: bedofroses@xtra.co.nz Web: www.bedofroses.co.nz
Cell: 0274-949-062

Freshly-brewed coffee and a home-baked chocolatey delight in hand, I squidged into the comfy cream sofa and listened to Louisa as she reeled off their legendary breakfast menu. As delicious as it is elaborate, everything is home-made from the bread and the blueberry muffins to the pancakes with berries and passion fruit curd, all served out on the terrace with panoramic views to the hills and woods just outside town. As the name suggests, everything here is designed for your sheer comfort and delight. Great beds, crisp white linens and fluffy towels are the guest stars in elegant rooms full of country-style French antiques, gorgeous old oak chests, liberty prints and flowers. Kerikeri is a charming little town, the historic 'cradle of the nation' and full of bountiful orchards and greenery, evident in their tropical-flavoured garden, which yes, does have a bed or two of roses that are set among other flowery treasures brought over by early settlers. It's only a short walk to the shops and cafés or to the picturesque river basin with its yachts, historic buildings and Maori heritage. Enjoy this place for as long as you can - a stay away from home will not find you in safer, more hospitable hands than these. The Hobson-Corrys are consummate hosts and it is a pleasure to welcome them back both to the North Island and to this guide.

Rooms: 3: 1 king and 1 queen both with en-suite showers. The Monet Suite has 1 queen with en-suite bathroom, living room and cooking facilities.
Price: $275 - $350 for rooms in house. Monet Suite (French Cottage) is $385 for 2pp and $60 per head above 2 not exceeding 3 in total. Fleur de Rose room offered with additional queen room at $480.
Meals: Full breakfast incl'. Good restaurants near by.
Directions: From Whangarei take SH1 north to Pakaraka. Turn right onto SH10 and travel 18km. Then turn right onto the Kerikeri Road. Bed of Roses is at the end of the village on the right past the Northland Technical Institute.

Chalet Romantica

Inge and Ed Amsler

6 Bedggood Close, Paihia, Bay of Islands
Tel: 09-402-8270 Fax: 09-402-8278 Email: info-chalet@xtra.co.nz
Web: www.chaletromantica.homestead.com/accom1.html
Cell: 027-226-6400

I don't think I can remember a place that offers so much for so little and I'm going to have to hurr
along to mention everything. Chalet Romantica marches into this book simply for Ed and Ing
whose warm natures and dedication to their guests mean the battle is won before the warship
set sail. Bedrooms all have sea-facing balconies, firm beds, crisp linen, strong massage showe
with adjustable heads, fridge, music-player, microwave, dial-out phone, TV, VCR, bathrobes, sm
bottle of bubbly, fresh flowers. Breakfast is Swiss-style which means soft-boiled eggs, mues
cheese, yoghurt, different types of bread… but less Swissish dishes like eggs Benedict or bacc
and eggs are also on the cards. There is a small swimming pool inside the house with an exerji
system that drives a current against which you can swim for fitness. They have "a bit of a farn
with goats and two acres of land and you can walk from the house into the bush. One of th
most impressive B&Bs I've ever visited and extraordinary good value. More is more. And let's n
forget the Chelsea Bride, the Amslers' 42-foot charter boat, which is described on the next pag

Rooms: 3: 2 king suites with kitchen-lounge and en/s shower; 1
queen with private shower.
Price: $145 - $285. Singles on application. You can book the
rooms without breakfast for $15 less per person.
Meals: Swiss-style breakfast included.
Directions: From Opua 5km towards Paihia down hill, turn L
into McMurray Rd, then 1st L into Bedggood Close, opposite the
tennis courts.

The Chelsea Bride

Inge and Ed Amsler

Opua Marina, Bay of Islands
Tel: 09-402-8720 Fax: 09-402-8278
Email: info-chalet@xtra.co.nz Cell: 027-226-6400
Web: www.yachtcharter.homestead.com/nz1.html

You landlubbers are missing out. The real beauty is at sea, where secluded islands and beaches can be explored in style aboard the Chelsea Bride. This roomy 42-foot sloop is where, as Ed says, "a bad day on the water is better than a good day in the office." He's seems to be right too. We sailed into the first misty day the Bay of Islands had seen in months, but I was still thrilled to be there, especially when lunch was served. This charter's menu is a foody's delight with three or four courses of gourmet cuisine. As I was tucking into Inge's mouth-watering chicken salad, I figured the Chelsea Bride would be hard to beat. Ed has held his skipper's ticket for 30 years, 25 of which have been in New Zealand, so his knowledge of the sea and the bay's history is comprehensive. The longer you're aboard, the further you'll venture, seeing diverse wildlife along the way. Everything you need is on board: snorkel, fins, an inflatable dinghy or kayaks to step onto land and explore the islands' scenic tracks. The double berth is private and comfortable, but I'd be inclined to sleep under the stars in the foredeck's luxury double hammock. If you'd prefer to avoid the evening sea's gentle rock, the Amslers can combine day trips with onshore accommodation, their own Chalet Romantica being the obvious choice.

Rooms: 1 private berth: double with en-suite shower.
Price: Peak season: $1,390 all incl. For two/three people. Mid-season: $1,090. Low season: $950. Day sailing with lunch: $890.
Meals: Full breakfasts, light lunches and 3/4 course dinners including wine.
Directions: Exact directions to the marina and berth will be emailed upon booking.

Decks of Paihia B&B

Phillip and Wendy Hopkinson
69 School Road, Paihia, Bay of Islands
Tel: 09-402-6146 Fax: 09-402-6147
Email: info@decksofpaihia.com Web: www.decksofpaihia.com
Cell: 021-278-7558

Phil, gregarious and cheerful even after an epic series of flight misadventures the previous night, escorted me into the upstairs lounge area and the question at the back of my mind was instantly settled: yes, Decks of Paihia does have a lot of decking. The front of the house is bordered by a long deck that appears to float over the wooded valley stretching down to the sea-shore beneath and ushers into the room a tidal wave of sunlight. On the bottom storey are the guest rooms, with their own private decks beside the lawn and swimming pool. Hosts of ceaselessly busy birds, including the striking crimson rosella parrots, live in the surrounding trees. The rooms are bright and airy, with local artwork and sumptuous bed linen providing splashes of colour. The guest rooms all have flat screen TVs, DVDs and fridges and in the lounge a collection of elephant-themed images and artefacts rather caught my eye. There is also a treadmill in the office space, along with a computer for guest use, but apparently nobody ever uses it - and why would they? Wendy and Phil love travelling, swapping stories and relaxing and they've created a great space for you to do all three in, with no more effort than a gentle stroll… and perhaps the occasional bend of the drinking elbow. *Broadband cord for laptops and internet computer available.*

Rooms: 3: all superkings with en/s bathroom with shower.
Price: $165 - $245.
Meals: Continental breakfast included.
Directions: From Opua 5km towards Paihia down hill, turn L onto School Road. Decks of Paihia is number 69. Street numbering out of sequence so continue to top of hill following odd numbers only.

Crow's Nest Villas

Marj Browning (Manager)
20 Sir George Back Street, Opua, Bay of Islands
Tel: 09-402-7783 Fax: 09-402-7783
Email: marj@vivid.net.nz Web: www.crowsnest.co.nz
Cell: 027-210-5242

With the Bay of Islands spread out beneath me, I counted the twinkling lights of the boats bobbing on the waters below the verandah at Crow's Nest Villas and couldn't imagine a nicer place to loiter as the twilight deepened. High on the hill above Opua harbour, the villas have spectacular views of the whole bay area. Both are immaculately presented with a nautical theme throughout that leaves you feeling refreshed rather than slightly queasy. There are ropes at the entrance, portholes for windows and even a 'welcome aboard' sign by the front door. The bedrooms are wrapped around with huge, unfolding French windows that face out into the blue and each has a glass wall to separate the en-suite bathrooms so that you can gaze out to the ocean as you wash. I could happily picture myself here padding around barefoot on the smooth qwilla-wood floors, flitting somewhere between the huge, comfy decks, open-planned living spaces and the yachting harbour and wharf below. Added to all this, Marj is a delightful and naturally caring person and is always at the ready to help with any queries. This is a great holiday pad that has all the necessaries, including TV, Internet and a complimentary bottle of wine, to make you feel right at home... but on holiday.

Rooms: 2 villas: Sails Villa has 1 queen and 1 twin both with en/s shower; Bridge Deck has 2 queens both with en/s shower. Both villas now have wireless internet connection.
Price: $215 - $545. Maximum 5 guests per villa.
Meals: Fully self-catered including BBQ facilities.
Directions: Ask when booking.

The Boathouse

Angie Kyriak
5 Beechy St, Opua
Tel: 09-402-6800; freephone in NZ 0800-683-722
Email: info@theboathouseopua.com Web: www.theboathouseopua.com

This is the coolest of wharf conversions, more boat than house, water constantly lapping beneath its prow. The Boathouse is supported on poles in the Opua Harbour, next to the Russell ferry jetty so you can watch the boats come and go from your huge deck with its glass and metal rail (last boat at 10 p.m.). You can even fish from the deck of the lower apartment, The Landing. The two apartments sit one above the other, similar in style, although there seemed to be even more space in the topmost living area, The Bridge, perhaps because the entire front wall slides away making the deck an extension of the room itself. The interiors are state-of-the-art, chic, shiny-new, lots of blue and glass, the nautical theme subtle and atmospheric (rather than obvious and annoying). And the kitchens have everything, including ice-makers. Basics like milk, tea and coffee, olive oil, washing powder etc are all provided, so all you need are the main food items and away you go. Right next door, by the way, are the Opua General Store which has a great bakery and restaurant. Other mod cons are a full entertainment system, large screen LCD TV, washing machines and clothes dryers, air-conditioning and wireless broadband. You will live luxuriously well at The Boathouse and all the boat and bird activity make its unique position in the heart of the harbour fascinating.

Rooms: 2 flats: The Landing has two double rooms; The Bridge above has one double room with en-suite shower and one office with fold-out queen-size bed.
Price: $550 (1st Oct – 1st April) for either apartment. $385 off-season. $100 surcharge from 1st December to 15th January.
Meals: Self-catering. Meals can be provided by prior arrangement. BBQ facilities on decks.
Directions: Right next to the car ferry in Opua. Call 10 minutes prior to arrival to alert the owners.

The Rocks Bed & Breakfast

Janice and Tim Langman
56 Great North Road, Kamo, Whangarei
Tel: 09-435-4676 Fax: 09-435-4676
Email: info@therockskamo.co.nz Web: www.therockskamo.co.nz
Cell: 027-651-3303

While sipping coffee on a misty morning, watching the sheep dogs playfully sprint around the lemon trees, I said to myself: "The Rocks, now there's an understatement." You'll understand when you wander through the white picket gate and enter the shaded canopy of the totara and walnut trees, for they veil a gorgeous outcrop of, well, rocks. These QEII-protected formations are extraordinary and their volcanic origins provoke much discussion about time and age as theirs is a mystery. Some geologists say they're 40 million years old, others say four million. It's easier to ponder the homestead's history. Tim and Janice have carefully renovated the 1922 kauri and totara house, giving considerable consideration to its origins. Aside from luxuries like fine linen, DVDs and flat screens, the rooms retain that charming homestead feel. Given a choice, ask for the splendid Jounneaux Suite, named after one of the young settlers who mischievously etched his signature into the window-pane. The dining room also retains its 1920s grandeur with furniture, wallpaper, sash windows, an open fireplace, a great baronial oak table and a petite cigar room, all from the Jounneaux era. Hearty rural fare is on the menu here, but good restaurants are close and Tim offers a ride to and from some personally-recommended eateries. Personally I would stay in, finding the company of the salt-of-the-earth Langmans a far more inviting alternative.

Rooms: 3: 1 double with en/s shower. 1 king room and 2 king-singles room; both share detached bathroom with bath/shower, but both rooms only rented to individual parties at one time.
Price: $130 - $225.
Meals: Full breakfast included. Evening meals $40 - $55, by arrangement. Good NZ wines available at additional cost.
Directions: Stay on SH1 heading north of Whangarei (DO NOT turn off to Kamo at the roundabout). Carry on past the rail over bridge and before the corner where the Kamo bypass rejoins SH1, look for white picket gate and The Rocks' sign, easily spotted from the road. A detailed map is on website.

Map Number: 1

Entry Number: 13

Breakaway Retreat

Mark and Sheelagh Prosser
1856 Whangarei Heads Road, McLeod Bay, Whangarei
Tel: 09-434-0711
Email: breakaway@breakawayretreat.co.nz
Web: www.breakawayretreat.co.nz Cell: 021-0262-2457

Stepping into Breakaway Retreat is like clambering into a tree-trunk hideaway. Tucked away just above the seashore, surrounded by native bush and singing with birds, this self-catering cottage is a sylvan idyll, newly built by Mark and Sheelagh entirely out of pinewood. The walls have been left simple and bare - the view and the trees are your three-dimensional works of art here. The cottage windows open onto the trees and to the seashore below and, lying on the bed in the main bedroom, I was comforted by the sounds of birds plashing in the water. You can stroll across the lawn to the shore and perch yourself on moeraki boulders (unusual to find them outside the South Island), or take the kayaks out for a splash. Alternatively, one could always watch DVDs on the huge TV in your living room; or I quite fancied the idea of indulging myself in the enormous two-person spa bath. Mark and Sheelagh lived in the cottage themselves last winter to see for themselves what would be needed to create a perfect home from home; so I doubt you will be at a loss for anything during your stay. Despite the feeling of rural seclusion, Breakaway is perfectly situated for further exploration of the Whangarei Heads area if you are feeling adventurous. Otherwise the Prossers' secluded beach (safe for children) offers endless opportunities for swimming, beach-combing, fishing and general pottering. Oh, and keep an eye out for dolphins and orcas from the deck between August and December.

Rooms: 2: 1 king, 1 twin, sharing bathroom with spa bath and shower. Open-plan living area and kitchen.
Price: $250 - $290. $45 per additional person.
Meals: Fully self-catering. Complimentary breakfast basket supplied on first day including fresh eggs from the resident chooks.
Directions: Follow signs from Whangarei to Town Basin and then to Onerahi. By Hammer Hardware turn L onto Whangarei Heads Road. Follow this road until you reach the McLeod Bay 50km speed sign. 2nd entrance on R after the sign.

Ara Roa

Paul and Susanne Olsen

Harambee Road, Taiharuru
Tel: 09-436-5028 Fax: 09-436-5028
Email: pvista@xtra.co.nz Web: www.araroa.co.nz
Cell: 021-293-5981

Susanne and Paul add a surcharge for one-night stays at Ara Roa and you'll kick yourself all the way back down the mountain if you have to pay it! The cottage is at the very top of a kilometre of exciting driveway… next stop heaven. Time to wheel out some of the big-gun adjectives: magnificent, awe-inspiring, breath-taking. That sort of thing. From the deck the world is laid out below you, miles of grassy hills and fields, until the mountains finally drop into the sea. The muffled roar of distant surf wafts up the mountain and envelops you. I sat staring until darkness forced me to evaluate my living quarters. Given the token price put upon it I suggest you try and book in for a year. Everything is hard to get out of… the bed, the bath, the shower, the beanbag in front of the Sky-linked telly. Walls are enlivened with colourful pieces of art you want to walk off with (like the blue fish sculpture in the main bedroom). Mod cons include a complex series of spotlights, phone (mobile coverage is perfect), very functioning kitchen, hi-fi, video, board games. Kayaking in the estuary sounds great, sting rays commonly seen. Or cockle-fossicking. Or next-door's farm is a big hit with kids. This is a fantastic find and may well be difficult to get into. You will thank me (and the wonderful Olsen family of course!) if you do.

Rooms: 1 guest house: 2 bedrooms sharing 1 double bath and separate shower. There's a separate studio apartment with 1 king and en/s shower, close to the main house for more guests if required.
Price: $250 - $350 per couple. $50 per extra person (i.e. 4 people would be $450). Surcharge for one night only $80.
Meals: Fully self-catering so bring your own breakfast etc. Dinners can be arranged with a bit of notice: $60 - $90. Breakfast provisions provided with high season rates.
Directions: Ask when booking.

The Shanty

Peter Sullivan
Cowan Bay Farm, 592 Cowan Bay Rd, Warkworth
Tel: 09-425-9550 Fax: 09-425-9553
Email: info.shanty@xtra.co.nz Web: www.cowanbayfarm.com
Cell: 021-045-1383

On a flat tidal rock bed, flanked by native bush, in a tiny private bay complete with a short sweep of sandy beach you will find an idyllic cottage, raised on stilts to allow high tide to lap beneath the deck. When I first laid eyes on it, all I could manage was a sigh and some goose pimples. The 'Shanty' was once genuinely a shanty, but it is a bit of a joke name now for this highly styly beachside retreat. Inside, polished kahikatea-wood floors are strewn with rugs, walls are white, russet timbers smell of wood wax. Deep couches flank a beautiful antique table scarred with age and French windows open wide onto a long deck built around ancient pohutukawa trees. The pantry is chock-full of provisions (herbal teas, spices, flour, sauces etc) and mod cons include a dishwasher, stainless-steel oven, microwave, outdoor BBQ, outdoor heaters... but no TV reception or phone here, although there are DVDs and a stereo for rainy days. The only sounds are the mud that pops or the herons that fish for snapper, like you can, five metres from the door. You can hunt for rock oysters, too. Two kayaks, life-vests and fishing gear are all provided. This place is so special that friends wonder why Peter doesn't live there himself. *Warkworth is 12 mins away. Children are welcome.*

Rooms: 2: 1 king, 1 queen and a queen pull-out sofa in the lounge, all sharing 1 shower room.
Price: $332 high season and 250 low season, for two. $50 for each extra person. Minimum two-night stay.
Meals: Self-catering only.
Directions: 50 mins north of Auckland. SH1 through Orewa, past Puhoi, up hill, along ridge, past Moir Hill Road on L. Right down Cowan Bay Rd (just past teddy bear sign on R). Go 6km and through farm gates. Pass barn and stock yards, L at T-junction to waterfront.

Peace and Plenty

Judith Machin

6 Flagstaff Terrace, Devonport, Auckland
Tel: 09-445-2925 Fax: 09-445-2901
Email: peaceandplenty@xtra.co.nz Web: www.peaceandplenty.co.nz
Cell: 021-665-661

Peace and Plenty faces the harbour, guarded by Old Albert, the giant Moreton Bay fig, and his attendant pohutukawa trees that make the green of this seaside village so impressive. The house is an elegant Victorian villa, built in 1888, a grand old NZ residence. You approach up the garden path beside tiers of lavender hedge and roses. Once inside, one's natural inclination is to follow the high-ceilinged central passage through to the breakfast room with its dresser of blue china. The breakfast table was elegantly laid out when I visited and laden with home-made muesli, lemon and poppy-seed cake and warm plum crumble. If it's not grown in Judith's garden, incidentally, most of the produce is local to Devonport. And then out onto the flower-laden back verandah, which overlooks a small but very well-designed tropical garden, a honey-pot for tuis, wax-eyes and wagtails. The house is made of original kauri with Marseilles roof tiles and corbelled chimneys. The rooms are very different and I liked them all, particularly those upstairs with their shuttered doors and little balconies overlooking the Waitemata Harbour and Mt Victoria: other rooms feature brass beds, Tuscan-tiled bathrooms and Victorian slipper baths. The Peace and Plenty is rightly held up as a high-water mark for Auckland accommodation and fully supports environmentally sustainable practices. Stanley the dog will willingly accompany guests on walks. *Ferry to City Centre and islands 2 mins' walk.*

Rooms: 7: 1 king en/s bath & shower; 1 king en/s shower; 1 king en/s bath and separate shower; 2 queens en/s shower; 2 superking/twin en/s shower.
Price: $230 - $350. Singles $200 - $265. Winter specials available.
Meals: Full breakfast including smoked salmon, scrambled eggs, waffles with warm berries or smoked bacon & maple syrup. In the evening, Devonport groans with eateries.
Directions: Ask when booking or see website.

Ascot Parnell

Bart and Thérèse Blommaert

St Stephens Avenue, Parnell, Auckland
Tel: 09-309-9012 Fax: 09-309-3729
Email: info@ascotparnell.com Web: www.ascotparnell.com

In following Thérèse and Bart around their ultra-modern, newly-built apartment I managed to fill all the white space I allow myself for notes and I cannot read the tiny scrawl that followed! This is a measure of how much there was to enthuse over. In a couple of broad statements I will say that your hosts could not care more enthusiastically about their guests. And that every practical detail of their B&B has been minutely considered from your point of view… and only the highest quality has been sought in all things. All is super-modern, with the large, open living space drawing your eye - and your entire body - out to the balcony for the city view. There is much solid wood, pebbles in pot plants, marble in bathrooms, thick glass showers, mirrors, modern art, warm simple colours, perfect white linen on new beds. Mod cons include an open-plan kitchen with a coffee-maker and free juice, there's a Mac for guest use (Airport available throughout the apartment for those that understand) and guests have access to a heated swimming pool, security-swiper for the lift, underground parking, CD player, laundry… I mean, the list is endless. It is a beautifully decorated, slick, well-organised but always homely flat. Thérèse and Bart, who were once Belgians (French, German, Flemish/Dutch spoken), live in the adjacent apartment with Khalifa, their aristocratic and well-mannered saluki, and will make absolutely certain you are well looked after. *Bart also offers a cheery airport pickup service.*

Rooms: 3: 2 garden-view queens with en-suite shower; 1 super-king suite with harbour view, en/s shower and separate bath.
Price: $225 - $385. Singles $195 - $295.
Meals: Full breakfast included. On occasion if raining hard suppers can be arranged but Parnell is restaurant heaven.
Directions: Ascot Parnell is only 1.5km from Downtown/Central Business District. Please call to ask for full directions when booking.

Braemar on Parliament Street

Susan and John Sweetman

7 Parliament Street, Auckland
Tel: 09-377-5463
Fax: 09-377-3056
Email:
braemar@aucklandbedandbreakfast.com
Web:
www.aucklandbedandbreakfast.com
Cell: 021-640-688

Living history pervades Braemar on Parliament Street. Positioned next to the site of a sacred Maori spring, this 1901 townhouse shares its space with some of the oldest colonial parliamentary buildings in town. In 1994 Sue and John pooled everything they had to buy the house and save it from circling developers and demolition. Now, to walk through its doors is to step back in time to a house dressed in late-Victorian elegance and filled with bygone charm. A grand old kauri staircase leads to high-ceilinged rooms set with antiques and refined bathrooms with check-tiled floors and claw-footed baths. Old photographs line the walls upstairs while downstairs in the rose dining room you'll use silver cutlery to eat your delicious breakfast off fine bone china on white damask tablecloths. I spent the night in the Batten Suite, its rooms often visited by the 1930's aviation star Jean Batten during the years her father lived there. With even more character than their home, your hosts are as incredibly helpful as they are charming and will match your interest in the city and the house with as much information as they can. Sue loves to sing. You'll no doubt hear her hum to the sounds of the new day as she prepares breakfast, and John, who does voice-overs for TV and radio, is a natural-born raconteur. Braemar is as much a place to curl up on the sofa and read as it is a base from which to explore the city and you'll be sure to find both equally rewarding.

Rooms: 4: Batten Suite has 1 queen with en-s bath and shower and private living area; 1 queen and 1 double sharing bath and shower; 1 queen with private bath, house bathroom available for early arrivals.
Price: NZ$225 - NZ$350. Singles NZ$180 - NZ$295.
Meals: Great choice of full breakfasts included in price. Picnic lunches can be ordered on booking. Prices vary accordingly.
Directions: Emailed or faxed on booking.

Omahu Lodge

Robyn and Ken Booth

33 Omahu Road, Remuera, Auckland
Tel: 09-524-5648 Fax: 09-524-5108
Email: info@omahulodge.co.nz Web: www.omahulodge.co.nz
Cell: 021-954-333

We stumbled into Robyn and Ken's breakfast room at an unseasonably early hour on our way to the airport, and were greeted by just the kind of breakfast to set you up for a day – or two – and the sort of welcoming hosts that we love. Robyn and Ken have been pretty much everywhere (although the Great Wall of China is still on the to-do list) and have amassed a whole host of *objets d'art* and travellers' tales. Their best collection, though, is Kiwi through and through: an assembly of mottled kauri-wood furniture that the museums are dying to get their hands on. Upstairs, the Omahu Room has the kind of window-seat I dream of snuggling up on with a book. The Mt Hobson and One Tree Hill rooms give views of, you guessed it, Mt Hobson and One Tree Hill, with fresh white walls and bright paintings on the walls. The glass brick wall of the bathroom makes the space seem even brighter. My favourite, however, was the Pool Suite downstairs, with its separate lounge with cream walls, tapa cloth and en-suite bathroom (I'm always one for a luxurious bathroom) which has a glass wall looking through to some enclosed fernery, a sort of bush bath in the middle of the city. All the little things have been taken care of here, with a thousand thread count sheets, rattan furniture for relaxing by the courtyard pool, and four hot-water cylinders so that they never run out of hot water!

Rooms: 4: 1 king with en/s shower; 1 super king/twin with en/s shower; 2 queen with en/s shower.
Price: $160 - $295.
Meals: Great choice of full breakfast from an extensive menu. Good-quality restaurants within easy walking distance.
Directions: Traveling either north or south on the Southern Motorway (State Highway 1), take the Market Road exit. Travel east and continue to Remuera Road. Turn R, then R again into Omahu Road. Omahu Lodge is on the R.

Rapaura Water Gardens

Sacha and Sally Sank

586 Tapu-Coroglen Rd, Thames
Tel: 07-868-4821
Fax: 07-868-4821
Email: info@rapaura.com Web: www.rapaura.com

Seven waterfalls cascading over black granite boulders through dense rainforest into deep clear pools – aka 'The Seven Stairs to Heaven'. Here are 64 acres of private paradise for you to explore at your leisure. Further down, the creek weaves and gurgles through rambling gardens, past native trees, exotic flora and Monet-esque lily ponds. "The best garden is a well-kept wilderness," is one of the sayings at Rapaura. This is especially true as the gardens have been restored to their former glory after being devastated by a 'weather bomb' in 2002. Semi-camouflaged by native tree-ferns the lodge combines antiques, bright colours and *objets d'art* from the owner's time in Hong Kong. I loved the bold Chinese calligraphy that greets you when you enter and cooed over the porcelain elephants bearing potted ferns in the soothing setting of the breakfast room. I stayed in the cottage where I found every creature comfort had been taken care of, from extremely comfortable sofas and bed to top-quality linens and fresh coffee in the kitchen. We ate a delicious dinner in the lodge, eating in the dining room with its full-length sliding doors looking out onto the wilderness below. Simply put, an amazing place. Sally and her son Sacha have also opened Koru at Rapaura, an inviting café serving all their home-cooked favourites with rare NZ flavours you'll struggle to find elsewhere. Local art is also displayed on site.

Rooms: Lodge: 2 queens with shared bath and shower. Cottage: 1 queen with bath, shower and toilet. Lodge and Cottage are self-contained.
Price: Lodge: $275 for two and $65 per extra person. Cottage: $165 for two, $45 per extra person.
Meals: Continental breakfast provisions included. Dinner available by prior arrangement.
Directions: From Thames take the road toward Coromandel. At Tapu turn right toward Coroglen and Whitianga. Follow signs to Rapaura, 6.5km on the right.

Map Number: 1

Entry Number: 21

Driving Creek Villas

David Foreman

21a Colville Road, Coromandel Town
Tel: 07-866-7755 Fax: 07-866-7753
Email: info@drivingcreekvillas.com Web: www.drivingcreekvillas.com
Cell: 021-116-6393

It was on these very banks of the Coromandel stream that gold was first discovered in New Zealand. Some 150 years later, I struck gold myself... in the form of the Driving Creek Villas, three comfortable retreats tucked away amongst trees and native bush. David has designed everything to lull you into a state so hypnotically tranquil that no matter how long you spend here it will never quite seem enough. Once you step inside, the villas are so fresh, airy and naturally uplifting that you'll feel as if you're floating within their light wooden structures. With polished wooden floors, sprightly orange and purple furnishings, chrome-fitted kitchens and French windows that bi-fold onto the deck, they ooze from all the right places that understated style of laid-back modern living. And you'll not want for comfort with the finest Egyptian cotton linen on beds and all the gadgets you could dream of elsewhere. But I'd forfeit them all simply to wallow in the Japanese hot tub and listen to tui birds sing over the sound of the stream. Kids and opportunists alike will love exploring the creek to feed the eels (!) and search for gold. There's also the famous Driving Creek Railways, a gold stamper battery and two beautiful gardens right at your door and with stunning beaches and walks all around you can happily idle your way through a lazy weekend or more. *Bicycles are complimentary. Renowned for its artsy community, the village and its lovely restaurants are minutes away.*

Rooms: 3 villas: all have 1 queen and 1 twin sharing a bathroom; two have Japanese hot tubs.
Price: $275 - $295. Extra person $39.50.
Meals: Fully self-catering. The Driving Creek Café is a short walk away.
Directions: Drive 2km north of Coromandel township, where the road forks take the left-hand Colville Road turning. Driving Creek Villas are 200m past here on your left over the one-lane bridge.

Kuaotunu Bay Lodge

Lorraine and Bill Muir

8, State Highway 25, Kuaotunu/Wharekaho, RD2 Whitianga
Tel: 07-866-4396 Fax: 07-866-4396
Email: muir@kuaotunubay.co.nz Web: www.kuaotunubay.co.nz
Cell: 027-601-3665

Turning your back on the views at Kuaotunu might well be the hardest thing you have to do on your holiday. I longed to stay to watch the sun set and the moon rise, but needs must when the devil drives and I had to press on. The house is perched above the beach among ten acres of garden, its wrap-around decking offering up a panoramic spread of sparkling sea, white sand and open expanse of sky for your delight. Think of a picture postcard and, unlikely as it sounds, you are probably there. There's no need to move when such a view is available, so grab a meal from Whitianga or Coromandel Town, bring it back to your private deck and enjoy the view. It's worth trying out the rest of the house, though, because Lorraine and Bill milled the macrocarpa and built it especially for guests, with an open-plan layout that cleverly allows you to be just as sociable as you choose. I was fascinated by the collection of objets trouvés scattered throughout the house, such as the child's raincoat made from woven reeds, or the collection of model Pacific Island boats from Bill's childhood. The guest rooms are similarly appealing spaces, with the strong colours of local artists' work competing for attention with the bright sunlight and the sea views. If one should want to venture further afield than the beach below, then the hotspot (literally) of Hot Water Beach is within driving distance, and the artistic community of Coromondel offers a great day trip.

Rooms: 3: 1 twin with shower/bath across hall, 2 queen with en/s shower.
Price: $250 - $275
Meals: Full breakfast included. Recommend picking up something and bringing it back. The Coromandel Smoke House in Coromandel Town is worth a trip.
Directions: Take the SH25 18km north from Whitianga to Kuaotunu. Kuaotunu Bay Lodge is clearly signed on the road.

Map Number: 2

Entry Number: 23

Hahei Oceanfront

Raewyn and Joe Whitham

23 Wigmore Crescent, Hahei, Whitianga
Tel: 07-866-3199 Fax: 07-866-3198
Email: info@haheioceanfront.co.nz Web: www.haheioceanfront.co.nz
Cell: 0274-753-301

I arrived early and made my usual bumbling English apologies, but Raewyn and Joe were totally unperturbed. Within minutes we were settling down with good coffee and Raewyn's home-made and wickedly moreish shortbread. We sat in the centrepiece of this minimalist home, a huge lounge with white sofas and day-beds, lined on most sides with local art and with a huge deck with views down to the beach only yards away. It really is the most stunning setting and the house an architect's delight, even more picture-perfect than its photograph suggests. My room was simply but skilfully turned out with beautiful framed photos of nearby Cathedral Cove on the walls and a multitude of pillows and cushions piled on the bed. The en-suite bathroom caught my eye too, with its border of paua shells set into the tiles and the ocean-green sink raised above the counter. Even swankier than this, the Whithams are particularly, and rightly, proud of the suite, with its living room and deck and 180-degree views. There's a new, well-protected courtyard with an outdoor fireplace and it catches every last ray of the setting sun, should you want a change from sundowners on the deck. Raewyn and Joe are perfect hosts and will gladly fill you in on the best spots to dine, boat and bathe on the peninsula. Back at the house later that night, I stepped outside to marvel at the clearest of night skies, full of stars, before falling into bed and being lulled to sleep by the soft crumping of ocean waves.

Rooms: 3: 1 suite with king and en/s bath and shower; 1 superking/twin with en/s shower; 1 king with en/s shower.
Price: $250 - $370 (high season Mahurangi room) for rooms, $725 for the suite. Singles $30 less. Minimum 2-night stay in rooms between 20/12 and 31/03. For the suite there is a 2-night minimum year round.
Meals: Full breakfast included.
Directions: From Tairua follow SH25 and turn right into Hot Water Beach Road. Follow signs to Hahei. First right into Pa Road, then first left into Wigmore Crescent. House at end of crescent on right.

Hot Water Beach B&B

Gail and Trevor Knight

48 Pye Place, Hot Water Beach, Whitianga
Tel: 07-866-3991; freephone in NZ: 0800-146-889 Fax: 07-866-3291
Email: tknight@xtra.co.nz Web: www.hotwaterbedandbreakfast.co.nz
Cell: 0274-799-620

The draw cards for the tiny beach-village itself are a spring-fed lagoon and the rare hot-water springs that bubble up beneath the sands of the tidal zone. At low tide you go out, dig a hole in the sand and wallow in your own home-made hot bath. This is even more extraordinary at night and Trevor and Gail know about the tides and will provide spades and wine. Not many B&Bs provide spades and wine. You will be hard-pressed to find fault with this place. I tried, but failed. The vital elements of bedrooms and bathrooms are immaculate with any trimmings you might dream up (shower-caps, PC plugs, extra blankets) already thought of and covered. Downstairs: a full-size snooker table with an (honesty) bar and telly for blokesy sports occasions. For the beach: boogie boards, beach towels and, of course, spades to dig your bath. Breakfasts are enjoyed together in the open-plan sitting-room-kitchen-deck with a full wall that opens towards the beach. The house is fresh, modern, beachy with loads of space, neat tubs of aloes on gravel paths, wooden decks, one bearing an outside hot tub which looks out to sea. And to top it all Gail and Trevor are just incredibly nice and natural, committed to your happiness. AND the rates make very pleasing reading. The 4-night maximum stay in operation here gives others a turn! Roxy the foxy dog and Pipi the tabby cat are the animals in situ.

Rooms: 2 queens with en-suite shower.
Price: Doubles $200 - $320.
Meals: Full breakfast included.
Directions: From Tairua follow the SH25 north. Turn R into Hot Water Beach Rd. Follow for 8km, bearing R at intersections & following signs. After 2nd single-lane bdge, bear L into Pye Place. House on R but go past & U-turn to make it up steep drive. Concise directions emailed on request.

Map Number: 2

The Mussel Bed B&B and Cottage

Chris and Paul Hopkins
892 Purangi Road, Cooks Beach, Whitianga
Tel: 07-866-5786 Fax: 07-866-5706
Email: welcome@musselbed.co.nz Web: www.musselbed.co.nz

The newly-built Mussel Bed is just a short walk from the white sands of Cooks Beach and its 3km crescent of safe swimming. And there can be no better place to wash off the salt than at Chris and Paul's B&B. The three guest rooms, in a separate wing of the main house, have been decorated in distinctive themes and blessed with many little extra touches, such as fresh brownies, jars of sweets, coloured scarves in the wardrobes and bonsai plants. The Victorian room with its fine floral china tea set was influenced by a stint in the UK, while the Pacifica is awash with regional paintings and wall hangings and a Koru symbol in the bathroom. The Beach Hut is ideal for four friends travelling together, with a queen downstairs and a loft room with twins. Each room has a large window-seat and a deck overlooking the rock garden; and this is where Chris will bring your breakfast (assuming you don't want it in bed), complete with fresh coffee, home-baked bread and her sumptuous home-made, honey-drizzled muesli. Paul is equally 'hands-on'. A tiler by trade, he's responsible for the glories of the bathrooms, while much of the furniture was made by a neighbour using recycled kauri from an old homestead. Coromandel adventuring starts here. Diving, fishing and shellfish all five minutes' walk away. Or take the kayaks down the stream to the beach. *Cathedral Cove and Hot Water Beach 10 mins by car.*

Rooms: 3 rooms in B&B guest wing: 2 queens with en/s showers, & 1 queen & 2 singles sharing shower; self-contained cottage: 1 queen & 2 singles sharing shower.
Price: B&B Guest Wing $175 - $275 per couple. $50 per extra person. Singles $150 - $250. Self-contained cottage $150 - $275 per couple with 5-night min stay during peak periods. $50 per extra person.
Meals: Continental breakfast included. Breakfast provisions are provided in the Cottage for 1st night only. Meals can be provided with prior arrangement.
Directions: 20 mins north of Tairua on SH25 R into Hot Water Beach Rd. Follow 2km then bear L into Purangi Rd signed Cooks Beach/Ferry Landing. Follow 9km & Mussel Bed 200m on R past tennis courts.

Entry Number: 26

Map Number: 2

Matawha

Jenny Thomson
61 Matawha Rd, Ruapuke, Near Raglan
Tel: 07-825-6709 Fax: 07-825-6715
Email: jennyt@wave.co.nz

My directions told me to go straight across the road into Matawha. This confused me somewhat as all I could see in front of me was a field. Which appeared to be full of cows. Showing the great pioneering spirit of my British ancestors I ventured forward and at the end of the field, Matawha suddenly loomed in front of me with beautiful wild gardens and flowers abounding. The house does not disappoint. From the infamous double room complete with piano and binoculars to the studio with spa and obligatory candles for atmosphere everything is welcoming and homely. At sunset you can sit in the spa, roll back the windows and gaze out to the sea or the mountain – whichever takes your fancy. You have the run of Jenny's 900-acre cattle and sheep station and you can tramp down past her horses, over the paddocks to five kilometres of possibly the best surf beach in the Southern Hemisphere. Jenny is an extremely well-travelled and knowledgeable lady, having spent time in Jordan, Europe and South America, often as a boffin on bovines (cattle expert). She'll also spoil you rotten with a groaning table of wonderful food, much of it from the Matawha organic vegetable garden. You'll not find anywhere else like this in New Zealand. *Raglan, Bridal Veil Falls, Waitomo Caves, horse-riding, hot water beaches and gardens are all nearby.*

Rooms: 3: 1 double with private shower; 1 twin room and 1 king studio sharing a bathroom.
Price: Doubles $120 - $150. Singles $60. Spa use extra. N.B. cash only!
Meals: Full breakfast included. Dinner $20 p.p. for 2 courses, lunch $15, BYO wine.
Directions: From Hamilton, west on SH23 for 28km, then L for Te Mata. R into Ruapuke Rd. 9.5km of road and track, keeping L. At Y-junction, L into Tuturimu Rd. Straight ahead 2km to T-jct. Straight across into Matawha.

Huntington Stables

Carole and Neil Wright
106 Maungakawa Road, RD 4, Cambridge
Tel: 07-823-4136 Fax: 07-823-4136
Email: info@huntington.co.nz Web: www.huntingtonstables.co.nz

Huntington Stables is so intelligently thought out for honeymooners that if you arrive as friends, don't blame me if you leave engaged. The wine cellar spoils you for choice, but perhaps try locally-born wine-maker Michelle Richardson's own drop? It's a wine typical of Carole and Neil in that they're supporting commendable New Zealand products and local businesses; in the eloquently self-contained and modestly-named Stables you'll find Essenza Coffee, Blue Earth toiletries, Antipodes Water, fresh local flowers and a bowl of fruit from one of the region's famous farmers' markets. The bathroom is a work of art and the kitchen will motivate even the weariest cook. But, if you're a foody, I suggest popping next door to the Wrights for a meal. The highlight for me was a home-made berry sorbet; it was Carole's first attempt at that dish, but evidently successful as Neil and I were re-filling our bowls as if we'd lived dessert-deprived childhoods. That evening, for research purposes only, I had a sauna, a swim in the pool and ozone-treated spa under a star-lit canopy that illuminated each wet foot print. The next morning, I woke to the sunrise and a view of the picture-perfect Mt Mangatautari, a silver disk of cloud hovering over its summit. And that's what the friendly Huntington Stables is like, a picture-perfect touch of class in a petite, pretty town.

Rooms: 2 lodges. North Stable: 1 superking or twin king singles with en-suite slipper bath/shower. South Stable: 1 king with en-suite slipper bath/shower.
Price: $390 - $450 per stable.
Meals: Full and continental breakfast supplies included. Dinner by arrangement for $65 per person.
Directions: See website for detailed directions and map.

Thornton House

Christine Manson and David Cowley

Thornton House, 2 Thornton Road, Cambridge
Tel: 07-827-7567 Fax: 07-827-7568
Email: info@thorntonhouse.co.nz Web: www.thorntonhouse.co.nz

I didn't want to leave idyllic Cambridge after David showed me his red 1963 MGB Roadster. Unfortunately I was short on time, but if you play your cards right, he might give you a ride to the supermarket via a distant open road. If you do head out, Thornton House is a welcoming place to return to. It was built of solid Coromandel kauri in 1902, around the same year the mighty pin oak was planted in the garden, which also nurtures over 100 roses, a protected magnolia grandiflora, a plentiful avocado tree and five healthy chooks who lay fresh eggs every day. Local gourmet restaurants are within walking distance, as well as a top fish-and-chip shop, so you can pick up a scoop of this iconic Kiwi tucker and bring it back to the private garden gazebo, which is equipped with speakers for a little musical ambiance. The Garden Room has a claw-foot bath and a bay window where you can sit in complete privacy with a complimentary cuppa and some home-made biscuits. But do make an effort to get out. Lake Koutu is literally just over the road and well worth an early-morning walk, when it's slightly misty and the trees are full of birds. Don't be scared to stretch out too, because Christine offers a relaxation massage service in your room, a great way to warm down.

Rooms: 2. Garden Room: 1 queen and 1 single with en/s bath and shower; Blue Room: 1 queen with en/s bathroom. Baby's cot and high chair available.
Price: Garden Room: $270. Blue Room: $225.
Meals: Full and Continental breakfast included.
Directions: See website for map and details.

Warm Earth Cottage

Gilbert and Anne Miller

Thompsons Track, Katikati, Bay Of Plenty
Tel: 07-549-0962
Email: romance@warmearthcottage.co.nz
Web: www.warmearthcottage.co.nz

The Millers are an industrious Kiwi couple that have gradually sourced recycled materials from the Internet and, with the help of award-winning interior designer Jacquie Bain, creatively fashioned two very eclectic, fun cabins. Forget that unnecessary newfangled electricity stuff. Gas barbecues and candlelight do more than simply set the mood here. There's also a free-standing potbelly stove that you should definitely light (I doubt you will be able to resist in fact) so you can listen to the embers crackle and smoulder while you drift off to sleep in some very fine linen. Silver goblets are on hand to sip Bert's wide variety of home-stilled chemical-free liquors. Select a complimentary bottle and head outdoors to the fire-heated slipper-bath tucked privately away beside your cabin, or on the deck if you prefer, where the verandah ceiling doubles as a blackboard with sweet messages left by the hands of previous travellers. One read: "if this is as good as it gets, then this must be heaven." I understood the sentiment down by the Waitekohe stream where the cicadas roar. There's a couple of shallow swimming holes, a fire-pit and hammocks strung under rewarewa trees where I met a young English couple head to toe in their own hammock; they stretched, gave me a wave and smiled as if to say "we have found the good life". They're right, of course. Life is very good here. BBQs, hot baths, bird song and a sense of humour to boot – take a peak at Bert's little tattoo on the back of his head… it'll bring a smile.

Rooms: 2 cabins with queens and separate/shared bathroom cabin. Both have private, outdoor fire-heated slipper baths.
Price: $200 for first night, $150 thereafter.
Meals: Complimentary BBQ breakfast provisions & bread/cheese/fruit platter provided. Evening BBQ provisions $80 for 2 (prawns, scallops, marinated chicken, salads, dessert).
Directions: From Tauranga take SH2; look for Morten Estate Winery, Thompsons Track 2km further. From north: 6km past Katikati towards Tauranga pass Pacifica Golf Course on L, over Waitekohe Stream bdge. Thompsons Track 1st on R. Look for sign further up rd.

Fothergills on Mimiha

Bev Fothergill

84 Mimiha Rd, Matata, Whakatane
Tel: 07-322-2224 Fax: 07-322-2224
Email: bev@fothergills.co.nz Web: www.fothergills.co.nz
Cell: 027-460-5958

Bev Fothergill, an ex-teacher with three children and four grandchildren, is clearly the nurturing type. And her sprawling garden, which was once part of the family farm, is testament to her abilities: crimson liquid-amber trees, flowering cherries, crab apples, orange persimmon, passion fruit, three types of apple, piles of pumpkins and feijoas. If you like freshly-grown food, you'll be as happy as a pig in mud; incidentally, there actually is a pig living here. Fothergills have farmed this spot for 42 years, hidden away in this "special, lovely little valley" (Bev's own incontrovertible words) with the Mimiha stream meandering through the garden. It was a balmy autumnal afternoon when I visited, perfect weather for an outdoor Mediterranean feast of mozzarella and heirloom tomato salad, all freshly picked from the garden. My only regret was that I didn't come on a summer's evening. With the patio lit by fairy-lights and flares, Bev's husband often plays his ukulele for guests and neighbours and the parties can go on into the wee hours. When guests retire, they can look forward to cosy rooms or the comfortable self-catering cottage. Either way the Fothergills' breakfast is not to be missed: freshly-squeezed juices, endless varieties of fruit, home-made Greek yoghurt, muesli, jams, jellies, preserves and probably the best toasted bagels in New Zealand… and it's all home-grown and fresher than a shower of summer sun.

Rooms: 2: 1 B&B suite with 1 queen room & 2 singles room with kitchenette & shared bathroom with shower downstairs; 1 s/c cottage sleeps 6 (1 queen, 1 bunk room, 1 sofa bed). Spa pool available.
Price: B&B from $160 pp for 2 sharing, $30 per extra person. Mimiha Cottage: min 2-night stay, $320 for 2, reduced tariff for weekly stay of $750. $10 per extra person.
Meals: Home-grown, home-made breakfast included. Evening meals by arrangement.
Directions: From Whakatane, take Thornton Rd past airport, then on thro Matata. 5km past Matata, L on to Mimiha Rd. From Tauranga/TePuke, follow SH2 turn into Mimiha Rd. Fothergills 840 m up road.

Map Number: 2

Entry Number: 31

Knapdale Eco Lodge

Kees and Kay Weytmans

114 Snowsill Rd, Waihirere, Gisborne
Tel: 06-862-5444 Fax: 06-862-5006
Email: relax@knapdale.co.nz Web: www.knapdale.co.nz
Cell: 0274-465-658

When I arrived Kay and Kees were sprucing up an already stunning Knapdale for the New Zealand 'House of the Year' assessment. (Incidentally they went on to win gold, just another acknowledgment to add to a long list of awards for accommodation and environmental achievements). Needless to say this 32ha sustainable farm is an absolute cracker. The Weytmans are aiming for complete self-sufficiency. This means that freshly-harvested veggies are served alongside home-grown beef, venison or lamb for dinner (you must experience one of Kay's four-course wonders); while orchard fruits, fresh eggs and home-made muesli make their entrance at breakfast. All the animals, the eels in the lake, the roaming deer and the penned porkers for example, are up for a bit of personal interaction so feel free to join Kees on a farm-feeding spree. Kees, a forestry man by trade, is utterly entranced by nature: "I'm in love with my trees!" he enthused, directing a flow of aborial information my way. Things to do here are as numerous as the thriving community of woody perennials. Knapdale is home to unique geological phenomena, is steeped in Maori history and supports a wide array of NZ wildlife. A multitude of shade-dappled strolls suitable for the lazy poets among us and endless trails suitable for the hardier hiker extend through the farm into the wild lands beyond, taking in caves, waterfalls and magical Maori spots. With Gisborne just 8km away this beautifully tranquil place could keep you entertained for weeks... or the rest of your life in the case of Kay and Kees.

Rooms: 2: 1 king with en-suite bath and shower; 1 king with private bath and shower.
Price: $303 - $363.
Meals: Full breakfast included. 4-course gourmet dinner by arrangement incl' pre-dinner drinks $75 pp.
Directions: Coming from Hawkes Bay on SH2, turn L at Makaraka, direction Opotiki/Auckland. Turn R 5km past Makaraka at green signpost saying: "Gisborne, via Mangapapa". Snowsill Rd is 1st L & Knapdale Eco Lodge is signposted. Coming from Gisborne: Snowsill Rd is last road on R before reaching SH2 on Back Ormond Rd.

Peach Gully Cottage

Kristal and Craig Foss

2006 Waimarama Road, Peach Gully, RD 12, Havelock North
Tel: 06-874-6009
Email: cottage@peachgully.co.nz Web: www.peachgully.co.nz
Cell: 021-566-701

The beautiful drive out towards Peach Gully reached its zenith as I crested the brow of a hill and beheld the tantalising spread of Waimarama Beach and Bare Island. Yet I remained just as impressed by the homestead a few hundred yards further on. The extraordinary 1914 shiplap gardener's cottage has been wonderfully restored so it maintains oodles of original character. The glowing rimu-panelled walls and rich matai flooring, all salvaged and locally-milled timber, provide a cosy cabin feel that's heightened by the fire in the lounge. (This seems to have hypnotised the sofa which waits patiently for you and a book to join it.) Every tiny detail has been closely considered from the old-school light switches and fine Egyptian cotton linen to an original claw-foot bath. The cottage was even moved to a new spot to ensure the sea views. Here you can swim in the heated pool, get active on the astroturf tennis court, dabble with a bit of pétanque or pop down the road to the beach for a surf. The tennis court is floodlit so, if you fancy a game at night, you don't have to rely on the moon..., although I am told that the night sky here is rather spectacular which explains Waimarama's Maori translation "moon on the water". They have even got a waterfall which I got very excited about. Kristal tells me that people love it, especially with the plunge pool and especially in summer. So there you go. You can hike to your heart's content and discover a few geological and Maori wonders on the way.

Rooms: 1 self-contained cottage with queen bedr'm, kitchen, bathroom & lounge. Serviced daily.
Price: $320 per night. Enquire about seasonal rates.
Meals: Full breakfast supplies included. Self-catering. It's possible to pre-order a starter pack of supplies at additional cost.
Directions: Follow signs to Waimarama from Havelock North. Travel to end of Te Mata Rd and turn R at the T-jct onto Waimarama Rd. Stay on Waimarama Rd over the Tukituki River, past the Trading Post Café. Ignore Maraetotara Rd and Ocean Beach turn-offs. The cottage is on your R on Waimarama Rd.

Map Number: 2

Entry Number: 33

Awahuri, Taupo Garden Lodge

William and Suzanne Hindmarsh

70 Hindmarsh Drive, Taupo
Tel: 07-378-9847; freephone 0800 HAMLET, 0800-426-538
Fax: 07-378-5799 Email: wehindmarsh@xtra.co.nz
Web: www.taupogardenlodge.co.nz Cell: 0275-531-253

This is a beautiful small fishing Lodge. William and Suzanne have lived at Awahuri, Taupo Garden Lodge for 43 years and in the process they've designed the garden, the furniture and even the house itself. Walking through three acres of mature and tranquil gardens - which include towering native trees, irises, camellias, rhododendrons, lily ponds, waterfall and an olympic-sized grass tennis court – it's easy to forget that you're close to the centre of town. The lawn slopes right down to the inviting, clear, blue/green waters of the Waikato River where guests can fish (if you catch one Suzanne will cook it up for breakfast), swim or simply admire the view. The famous Huka Falls are also only a twenty-minute walk from the house. The lodge is packed with oil paintings, Persian rugs and dark, native wood-panelling and in winter guests like to warm their feet by a vast stone-surround fireplace, cradling a glass of good wine in one hand (William knows a thing or two about wine) and enjoying the view out to the snow-capped mountains of the Central Plateau. Both bedrooms have views over the gardens and wooden beams in the ceiling. The Garden Suite has a double bay window and fridge complete with complimentary wine, and even a spare bedroom 'for the chauffeur'... I knew I'd forgotten something. Meals are usually taken with William and Suzanne, but for those who really want to feel they're on holiday, breakfast in bed is always an option.

Rooms: 2: 1 queen + single en-suite (Heron Suite); 1 super-king en-suite + small single/dressing room (Garden Suite).
Price: $275 - $325 per night, double and single. Extra persons $70. Kids welcome, rates negotiable.
Meals: Breakfast included. Dinner by arrangement for guests staying 2 or more nights: $65 - $85 per person. Selected wines available with meal for additonal cost of $10 - $15.
Directions: Just north of Taupo on State Highway 1, turn into Huka Falls Rd (Taupo Lookout entrance). Turn into Rangatira Park (Kahurangi Drive), then Hindmarsh Drive. Number 70 is on lower terrace with wrought-iron gate.

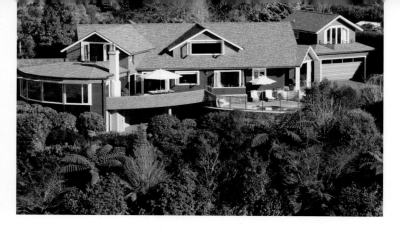

Scenic Heights Lodge

Mark and Sue Perry
24 Scenic Heights Drive, Acacia Bay, Taupo
Tel: 07-376-5866 Email: info@scenicheightslodge.co.nz
Web: www.scenicheightslodge.co.nz
Cell: Sue: 027-494-9873; Mark: 027-5713-402

Scenic Heights Lodge is relatively new, but its brief history is well worth mentioning: in 2003, it was purpose-built as a guesthouse by Gavin McDonald, the man credited with building the first five-star lodge in Taupo. It went on to win the House of the Year in 2004. In 2008, its run of good fortune continued when the disarming Sue and Mark, and Boots the cat, decided to move in, bringing their penchant for relaxed, friendly hospitality with them. Now the circumstances have come together to create a real gem of a guesthouse. From the living room, I could see Mr McDonald knew what he was doing; four sheets of glass dominate one wall and provide what must be one of the town's most encapsulating, panoramic, indoor, lake views. I was mesmerised by the scenery: the breeze gently pushing sail boats over the lake; trout-fishing locals patiently casting their lines, and the clouds rolling around Mount Tauhara in the distance. The balcony, where tuis and bellbirds occasionally zip overhead, is the perfect spot for Sue's alfresco breakfast and if you fancy a dip, test your level of fitness against the Exerjets in the pool. This is a welcoming, comfortable, peaceful place that's just a five-minute drive from town. It's even got the approval from a local morepork (a sort of owl), whose two-note tune you might hear at night, if you listen carefully.

Rooms: 3: 1 self-contained apartment, en-suite bathroom with shower; 1 superking, en-suite bathroom with shower; 1 superking, bathroom with bath and shower.
Price: $375 per night for studio apartment. $395 per night for either suite.
Meals: Breakfast included. Full and continental breafast provided for suites. Continental breakfast provided in studio apartment.
Directions: From Taupo, head north on Tongariro St and cross river (go 0.8km), left to Norman Smith St (0.7km), left to Acacia Bay Rd (3.5km), left to Scenic Heights (0.3km) to the Lodge at the end of the road.

Map Number: 3

Tauhara Sunrise Lodge

Rob and Becky McEwen

38 Mapara Rod, Acacia Bay, Taupo
Tel: 07-376-8555 Fax: 07-376-8557
Email: info@tauharasunrise.com Web: www.tauharasunrise.com
Cell: 021-728-875

Nestled into the side of a hill with sweeping lake views, the McEwens have quite a life. They've sampled most of the adventures and activities on offer in Taupo and can help you narrow down your choices. Just keep Friday or Saturday night free, because Rob and Becky offer a three-course meal, and judging from the perfectly-seared steak I devoured, it's an evening not to be missed. Nightly pre-dinner drinks are a must too, usually on the balcony beside the outdoor bar, or, on cooler evenings, in the lounge around a roaring open fire. Although if you've taken the aptly-named Chalet d'Amour you might become preoccupied. This funky private cottage is a honeymooner's dream; you can stargaze from its capacious bath by the window; or on the private rooftop pad, taking in some 180 degree lake views at the same time. If you're desperate to bring along the in-laws, the two rooms will accommodate them perfectly; they share a kitchen and each has a stylish en-suite bathroom, an entertainment system with a great selection of DVDs and full Sky satellite access. If your flight's taken its toll, Becky offers professional Swedish massage and will tenderise the toughest knots. Be sure to let Rob know what music takes your fancy. He's got a talent for hand-picking playlists and will pipe your preferred compositions through his internet-linked stereo, making you feel right at home in this friendly, relaxed, luxurious house.

Rooms: 3: Chalet d'Amour: 1 king with en/s with dual rainshowers, double spa bath, gas fire, & kitchenette; Lake Taupo: 1 queen, en/s bathroom; White Cliffs: 1 king or 2 twins, en/s bathroom.
Price: Chalet d'Amour: $575 per night. Lake Taupo: $300 per night. White Cliffs: $375 per night.
Meals: Continental or cooked breakfast included. 3-course dinner on Fri & Sat by arrangement.
Directions: Locate Acacia Bay Road. Proceed to Acacia Bay archway. After 400 metres, Acacia Bay Road veers left. However continue straight onto Wakeman Road, then turn right onto Mapara Road. Or see website for detailed directions.

Blue Duck Lodge

Dan Steele
Whakahoro, RD 2,
Owhango
Tel: 07-895-6276
Email:
dan@blueducklodge.co.nz
Web:
www.blueducklodge.co.nz
Cell: No cell phone reception

From the verandah I gazed up the steep horseshoe of cliff, bristling with native trees, which towers above Blue Duck Lodge. I stood stock still, revelling in a private concert of birdsong being performed with gusto before me. Tuis darted and flitted around the proud kahikatea across the river, a clear sign that Dan is making a difference here. He manages a natural and historic restoration project on 6,500 acres of Steele family land. Further progress can be seen within a short walk from the lodge, past the swimming hole and trout fishing spots, to rapids, where you'll find the eponymous – and protected - blue ducks thriving. There are kiwis here too; you might hear them calling if you listen carefully at night from the wooden lodge, a place that feels appropriately natural and harmonious with the environment. The lodge is simple, but modern and very welcoming, especially if you've come in from a day of trekking over hilltops with views of Ngaruhoe and Ruapehu; or from one of the Maori *pa* sites; or to the historic Bridge to Nowhere. If you want more, just ask Dan about trout-fishing, horse-trekking, kayaking, jet-boating and hunting possums, goats, deer and pigs. Blue Duck Lodge offers an authentic New Zealand experience with a genuine "hard-case" Kiwi bloke as your host. The land surrounding this isolated lodge is a rare and unique treat... New Zealand at its idyllic best.

Rooms: I lodge with 3 rooms: I queen; I superking which can be converted to two singles; I mezzanine that sleeps 4 with two single beds and a fold-out futon; I bathroom with shower.
Price: $120 for two. $30 extra per person. Minimum 2-night stay.
Meals: Fully self-catered, but breakfast supplies can be arranged for $20 per person: includes wild bacon and fresh farm eggs.
Directions: See detailed directions and Map Num on website.

Whare Ora

Diana and Tiri Sotiri
1 Kaha Street, Rangataua, Ohakune
Tel: 06-385-9385 Fax: 06-385-9385
Email: office@whareoralodge.co.nz Web: www.whareoralodge.co.nz
Cell: 027-481-5667

You are in the middle of the Tongariro National Park here, one of the first World Heritage sites ever to be declared. It is home to the Tongariro Alpine crossing, New Zealand's finest one-day trek. It's a magical world of lush rainforest, emerald lakes, purple desert, with an active volcano thrown in for good measure. No surprise, then, to discover they filmed *Lord of the Rings* here. Hundreds of walks, from 15 minutes to a week in length, and you can also canoe, mountain-bike, ski, horse-trek, fish, ride or read your book. At the lodge: huge rooms, peace and quiet, and piping hot baths to bring your feet back to life. The upstairs suite is enormous and has a vast triangle of glass through which Mt. Ruapehu provides a magnificent and ever-changing view. There's a wall of books, an open-plan sitting-room and a bed from which you can gaze out at the mountain. The downstairs suite is smaller but still has a bed with a mountain view and the most luxurious bathroom. I slept blissfully in crisp linen and awoke to the sound of birdsong. The house, originally built in 1910, is warm with lots of wood lending it a smart mountain-hideaway chalet feel. Log fires in winter and wine with Diana and Tiri before supper. They have a wide range of music and Tiri knows his jazz, too. *Scenic flights over the mountains available.*

Rooms: 2 suites; 1 with en/s spa bath and separate shower and 1 with en/s shower over the bath.
Price: Downstairs suite: $250 per night including breakfast. Upstairs suite: $325 per night including breakfast for two people. Extra person $70 per night (seasonal rates apply).
Meals: Full breakfast included. Dinner by prior arrangement only: $50 - $80 per person, dependent on the number of courses. includes wine.
Directions: East from Ohakune for about 5km, then left, signed Rangataua. Straight ahead for 0.5km, then left into Kaha Street. House on right at end of road.
Closed: Christmas.

River Valley

Brian and Nicola Megaw
Mangahoata Rd, Pukeokahu, Taihape
Tel: 06-388-1444 Fax: 06-388-1859
Email: thelodge@rivervalley.co.nz Web: www.rivervalley.co.nz

Long ago, when giant Moa birds stalked New Zealand's shores, a Maori adventurer named Hau went in search of his errant wife. The journey was long with many arduous river crossings. But most challenging of all was a torrent of water, which rose in the volcanic country of Ruapehu; Hau named the river Rangitikei, the day of the long walk. Fast forward to the late 20th century when in the spirit of Hau, Kiwi adventurers discovered that a lot of fun could be had hurtling down the Rangitikei in a rubber dinghy. These white-water rafting fanatics needed somewhere to stay, so River Valley was born. On the evening I stayed, damp-haired twenty-somethings drank with their rafting guide in the cavernous bar and restaurant, whilst the week-long art-course students discussed life drawing's finer points. After a meal of local chicken and warm chocolate and raspberry muffin, I walked back to my clutter-free room, with its rough-hewn furniture and neutral walls the colour of river pebbles. I climbed into my huge bed and dozed off with the gushing Rangitikei only metres away. Next morning was riding time. My pony was a feisty Arab... and it could go! Galloping up an escarpment overlooking the eternity of wild, volcanic country I felt a bit like Arwen from Lord of the Rings... except without the unearthly beauty or the fluent Elvish. After my GG visits I often hope to return; after one night at River Valley I am determined. *Golf, fly-fishing, Maori cultural walks and spa complex also available.*

Rooms: 8: 2 triples, 5 twins/doubles, 1 family with 2 bunks and 1 double. All with en-suite shower.
Price: $159 - $165 for whole room.
Meals: Continental and cooked breakfasts. Continental breakfast $10; cooked breakfast $15. Evening meals $45 for 3 courses and $32 for 2.
Directions: See website.

Cherry Cottage Homestay

Richard Aslett
Mangaweka Gallery and Homestay, State Highway 1, Mangaweka
Tel: 06-382-5774
Email: mangawekagallery@xtra.co.nz
Web: www.freewebs.com/mangawekagallery Cell: 027-526-6612

Mangaweka appears small, so remain wide-eyed, as since the highway was moved you may blink and drive straight past the township like I did. That said, not everyone zips past. Richard "Az" Aslett, an artist and Yorkshireman turned New Zealander, once stopped here for a coffee at the iconic Aeroplane Café. The short roadside break inspired him to buy a church and a cottage, both over 100 years old. Now the church is painted a bold yellow on the outside; inside an art gallery exhibits paintings, photography, pottery, sculptures, wood-turning and poetry from artists all over the country. In the garden, a cherry tree and other vibrant plant life flourishes wildly. "I leave it to do its own thing," Richard grins, although a part-time gardener, the free-roaming peacocks and affectionate 'Chicky' the chicken keep it reasonably tidy. The cottage is pretty simple, so if you're looking for rustic country charm, then this is the place. It's well priced, clean, comfortable and colourfully decorated. Richard will gladly cook, but prefers to recommend the Langholm Hotel just across the road; known for hearty pub grub, cold beer and locals who spin a colourful yarn; if you time it right, you might even see the Taihape Music Club playing there too, featuring Richard on drums. Cherry Cottage has a unique character in a town that Richard has embraced with his all his heart; his enthusiasm for Mangaweka is infectious, so allow for time, you just might end up staying.

Rooms: 2: 1 queen and 1 double, shared bathroom.
Price: Single $65 pp. Double $85. Queen $95. Whole Cottage $195 per night.
Meals: Continental breakfast included. Dinner available by request, 24 hours in advance, for $20 pp.
Directions: In Mangaweka, approx 28km North of Hunterville and 25km South of Taihape on State Highway 1. Look for distinctive yellow church and Mangaweka Art Gallery - Cherry Cottage is right next door.

Mairenui Rural Retreat

Sue, David & Matt Sweet & Leonie Taylor

1019 Ruahine Road, Mangaweka, RD54, Kimbolton
Tel: 06-382-5564 Fax: 06-382-5564
Email: mairenui@xtra.co.nz Web: www.mairenui.co.nz
Cell: 027-451-7545

Sweet land, indeed… a real hideaway in wild country, where a 200-foot gorge crumbles into the river below and cars pass by at the rate of one an hour. The Sweets farm the land as far as you can see on their side of the river and when David's father returned from Palestine in 1921, he built a rope-bridge across the gorge that still survives today. The views are inspiring, and exploring the Rangitikei River, the green sheep-mown hills, gorges and white cliffs of the area is irresistible. Mairenui is a way of life for Sue and David, not a slick business, and every crumbling outbuilding, painting or antique car has a story and a reason to be here. The land has not been overly manicured, just allowed to follow its nose. I saw a huge bush of never-pruned wild lavender, a willow bathing its branches in the lily pond, orchids growing from the tops of trees, wild turkeys strutting in the fields. You can stay in various places: the house, for traditional farmhouse B&B; the extraordinary architect-designed retreat with its awesome views of ridge and peak; or a cottage across the road surrounded by a ha-ha to keep the horses at bay. You're free to help on the farm, chop the wood, take to the hills. David and Sue are fabulous, well-travelled, humorous hosts, dinners at the homestead great fun. This is one of the great places to stay in New Zealand. *French and German spoken, golf and world-class fly fishing nearby.*

Rooms: The retreat sleeps 6 with bath and shower. 1 cottage (sleeps 10) with bath and shower. In house: 1 double with bath and shower; 1 twin/king with en/s shower.
Price: B&B in house $130 - $300 B&B per double; Retreat from $150 per double, $50 for each additional person; Villa $80 per double (accommodation only).
Meals: Full breakfast included if staying in the house. Breakfast provided at homestead for others $10 - $15 pp. 3-course dinner by arrangement $45 - $60 pp.
Directions: South for Mangaweka on SH1. Just before town sign, left for Rangiwahia on Ruahine Road. Down hill, over bridge, straight on along side of gorge for 9km and signed half way up hill on L.

Map Number: 3

Entry Number: 41

Queen Street Villa

Penny and John Pennington
27 Queen Street, Mt Victoria, Wellington
Tel: 04-971-6363
Email: book@queenstreetvilla.co.nz Web: www.queenstreetvilla.co.nz
Cell: 027-447-8131

The Pennington kids originally inhabited Queen Street Villa during university, but they trickled away with graduations, so Penny and John waved the renovating wand over it and now a student might feel inclined to leave his shoes at the door. Having said that, I spent my time horizontal on the sofa, watching cricket on the flat-screen and drinking beer! But don't get the wrong idea, this is a very chic private retreat where Penny's talent for interiors will make your stay feel rather special. The lounge is homely with its antique kauri chest, a flame mahogany chiffonier, bean-bags art works that certainly pleased this particular pair of eyes, and re-upholstered family armchairs that could stand as works of art themselves. Kimonos decorate the bedrooms, displayed over the ergonomically-designed Okooko beds, and there's even a pillow menu here – poor sleepers have no excuse. Penny and John offer airport pick-ups and will zip you through a quick tiki-tour namely up Mount Victoria to the best view in the city, although, if you feel like some air, the mountain trails are moments from your door. In fact most of Wellington's treats are accessible by foot. Queen Street is just ten minutes from Cuba Street, Courtney Place and the harbour. That said, the Penningtons' Miramar-based Chocolate Frog Café is well worth driving to for breakfast and hopefully you'll have time to chat with your delightful hosts there. And do try one thei coffees, which must rank among the very best in town.

Rooms: Villa has 3 bedrooms: 1 superking with en/s bath and shower fitting; 1 queen and 1 king that share separate bathroom with shower.
Price: For whole villa: $300 for first two people, $75 per additional person.
Meals: Cooked or any style of breakfast served at the villa, or complimentary breakfast at Chocolate Frog Café. Group dinners by arrangement.
 The Villa is very close to the city centre. From Oriental Parade head towards city but stay left to turn into Kent Terrace, then left into Elizabeth Street, right into Broughman, then left into Queen Street. The Villa is number 27.

South Island

South Island - Nelson

Adrift Beachfront Accommodation

Gordon and Bess Hampson and Emily and John Lolani
52 Tukurua Road, Golden Bay
Tel: 03-525-8353 Fax: 03-525-8353
Email: stay@adrift.co.nz Web: www.adrift.co.nz
Cell: 027-301-5832

The spectacular mountains that surround Golden Bay create quite a backdrop to this beach-set property. Gordon's beaming face was the first to greet me on arrival followed swiftly by the soothing tones of the sea. Here you are literally a pebble's throw away from Tukurua Beach, the Hampsons' own private slice of shell-peppered sands and gentle surf. Whales and blue penguins are known to frequent the tranquil waters while Einstein and Gracie (the family's two silver-haired cats) are more likely to be found hunting in the bushes. Adrift is the perfect launch pad to vibey Golden Bay's brimming culture of artists, Maori history and its multitude of walks and hikes. The brand-new self-catering cottages are elegantly finished in greens and dark woods with fully kitted-out kitchens, chic bathrooms (including all-singing-and-tap-dancing spa baths) and lavish beds which overlook the beach. Green-fingered and knowledgeable hosts Gordon and Bess have now turned their attentions to maintaining the natural wetlands, shore line and gardens, filling them with native species, encouraging the birdlife and ensuring that each cottage has its own pretty trail to the shore. A morning breakfast basket brims with everything local, fresh and home-made reinforcing the wonderfully wholesome family-run atmosphere of Adrift. *Kayaks and BBQ available.*

Rooms: 5 cottages: all king/twins with full kitchen, lounge, bedroom and bathrooms with double spa bath and shower. Additional pull-out bed available. 1 studio room: king/twin with en/s bathroom with shower.
Price: $108 - $450. $50 for each additional person.
Meals: Hamper of breakfast provisions included. There are over twenty restaurants in Golden Bay.
Directions: 18km north of Takaka on SH60. Adrift is signed on the right (Tukurua Rd), 2km past the Mussel Inn.

The Resurgence

Peter Adams and Clare de Carteret-Besson

The Resurgence, Riwaka Valley Road, Motueka
Tel: 03-528-4664
Email: info@resurgence.co.nz Web: www.resurgence.co.nz

The Resurgence is an environmental-award-winning lodge named after the source of the Riwaka River. This naturally-purified crystal pool springs from deep within the ground and is only half an hour's walk away, through land flourishing with native trees. The property borders Kahurangi National Park, home to a great variety of birds including keruru, bellbirds, fantails, wax-eyes, quails, pheasants and, my favourite, the jazzy-sounding morepork. Clare keeps a touch of the avian theme indoors too. Rachel Gilmore's beautifully depicted paintings of bellbirds, dotterel and whio feature in the Bush Suites. Nature lovers will be in their element here, especially with the doorstep opportunity to kayak and walk in the Abel Tasman, or over in Golden Bay on a private guided eco-tour, and then returning that evening to enjoy the good life at this terroir-style lodge, ideal for those who appreciate excellent cuisine and great conversation. I met the other guests over pre-dinner drinks and by the time we sat down for the main meal we were all pals and laughed away the evening. Clare's four-course meal of broccoli timbale, carrot, orange and ginger soup, a Mediterranean fresh fish main and a lime cream tart with espresso coffee was unfaultable... unlike Peter's jokes (just kidding Peter!). If you strike a rare rainy day, massage therapies, the Internet, CDs, a well-respected book exchange and shelves of bush suite DVDs are at your disposal.

Rooms: 10: 6 self-contained Bush Suites, 3 with kings/twins, en/s showers and 3 with queens and en/s showers. 4 Lodge Rooms, 3 queens and 1 king with en/s showers.
Price: $345 B&B to $745 B&B with dinner.
Meals: Breakfast, evening apéritifs & 4-course dinner for lodge guests included. Complimentary breakfast provisions provided for Bush Suites; 4-course dinner extra.
Directions: On SH60, drive thro Motueka then small township of Riwaka, then past 2 turns to Abel Tasman National Park. After 2km, at foot of Takaka Hill, take small turning L down Riwaka Valley Rd. Drive 5.7km until see sign for lodge on R.

Map Number: 4

Entry Number: 44

Atholwood Country Accommodation

Ian and Sarah Cole

118 Bronte Road East, Mapua, Nelson
Tel: 03-540-2925 Fax: 03-540-3258
Email: info@atholwood.co.nz Web: www.atholwood.co.nz

Atholwood once languished as a disintegrating bed and breakfast before it was blessed with its new and current owners, Ian and Sarah. They drastically renovated it into a contemporary, purpose-built, cedar lodge that caters for the most pernicity of travellers. The three suites were designed by Sarah, right down to the iconic ferns she has personally sewn into the sheets. Everything's there: a large shower, comfy king-size bed, robes, wireless Internet, full Sky, DVD and CD player. Atholwood also caters for young families with unpredictable, still-to-be-fully-socialised junior members, with the practical self-catering Gatehouse. It sits up the back of the rolling hillside section that quails, tuis, wood pigeons, pukekos and kingfishers all call home. The garden is ideal for games of spotlight, with paths snaking through native trees such as rimus and kowhais, and exotic plants like the alien-looking stagleaf fern. Beside the water's edge sits a saltwater pool, deckchairs and a jetty that looks like something out of the Wind in the Willows, with a picnic table hovering over the Waimea inlet, an estuary that completely ebbs away to mud, then magically floods again hours later. I sacrificed a sleep-in for this view. By leaving my curtains open, I faded into sleep admiring distant flickering lights over still waters; I woke to the sun strolling over the horizon and mildly casting a soft citrus beam into my window, as if to suggest: "life's good, get up and make the most of it."

Rooms: 2 suites with kings and en/s shower; 1 fully self-contained apartment with king and en/s shower; and the Gatehouse cottage at the entrance to the grounds which is self-contained with 1 superking and shower, and 2 queen rooms with a shared shower.
Price: Front suites $380 - $450. Gatehouse is $550 or $350 for downstairs, then $50 pp upstairs. (Note prices may increase from March 2010.)
Meals: Full complimentary breakfast with the B&B rooms, and breakfast provisions provided for the self-contained rooms.
Directions: From Nelson City, take SH6 past Richmond. Turn right in SH60. Continue 10 mins to Bronte Road East on R. 1km to Atholwood on R.

Istana Coastal Cottage

Sara and Bernard Isherwood

366 Coastal Highway, RD 1, Richmond
Tel: 03-544-1979 Fax: 03-544-1979
Email: info@istana.co.nz Web: www.istana.co.nz
Cell: 021-255-1555

Bernard's official title, he won't thank me for pointing out, is the rather impressive "Colonel Bernard William Ramsbottom-Isherwood (ret'd)". Yet (despite this) he and wife Sara could well be the most relaxed couple in this book. After returning from a stint in Malaysia, they've certainly found themselves a relaxing place to live. The Waimea Estuary stretches away in front of you to distant mountains while Rabbit Island pops up in the foreground. The table down by the water at the end of their property is a magical spot to sit and enjoy the evening. I could not believe that more houses hadn't encroached on the area, because as far as I could see, Bernard and Sara have this end of the inlet all to themselves. Lucky them. Istana means 'palace' in Malay and there is much asiatica in the guest cottage that sits in the garden near the house. It is built of rammed earth and is open-plan and high-ceilinged with lots of Canadian cypress, matai and rimu. There are Philippine armchairs made of vast bamboo poles, Chinese silk paintings and a fully-equipped kitchen, while big windows usher in floods of light. The Isherwoods say that the cottage is very popular with potters and painters and it's a great place to while the day away. I imagine picking some of the garden's grapefruit or feijoa, wandering down to the canoes and paddling, and nibbling for hours. *Swimming pool and tennis court. Children over 12 welcome.*

Rooms: 1 cottage: queen room and double bed sharing shower.
Price: $150 - $175 per couple. $25 per extra person.
Meals: Continental breakfast provisions provided (including free range eggs from the resident chooks). Self-cater for dinner or drive 8km to Mapua.
Directions: From Nelson, head towards the west on SH6. Turn north on SH60 towards Collingwood. Istana is 9.6km from that junction on the right. Emergency number 366.

Stafford Place

Bob and Sally Livingston

61 Redwood Rd, Appleby, Richmond
Tel: 03-544-6103 Fax: 03-544-6103
Email: staffordplace@xtra.co.nz Web: www.staffordplace.co.nz
Cell: 027-232-5121

Gracious among flowers, lawn and bird-filled agéd oaks, Stafford Place flaunts her authentic Victorian beauty. Built in 1866 as a replacement to the Redwoods' 1842 family home that originally fell prey to an earthquake, this house is steeped in history and stories - both of which your hosts will happily tell if you are interested. Surveyor Bob and wife Sally have inadvertently won an award for their restoration of the property since they moved here in 2000. The stately guest lounge, flushed with light from towering windows and filled with intriguing antiques, focuses on its skilfully-restored fireplace. With deep red walls and classic complimentary hues this is a room that warms in winter and cools in summer. I loved the bathroom, a whole suite in itself, with giant clear-sided shower, delicately-flowered walls and polished matai floor. It was also the cause of a good two-hour extension to my bedtime when I fell into a bubbly sleep in the claw-footed bath. Staying true to the traditional nature of the property Sally pulls out all the stops at breakfast with her home-made muesli and scrumptious kedgeree that will set you up, as it did me, for the whole day. You are free to roam the 10-12 acres of olive groves and farmland with welcoming golden lab Katie. And, with only the one suite, the peace and space are exclusively yours. Rabbit Island's secluded beaches are only a moment away.

Rooms: 2: 1 king with full en-suite bathroom and 1 single room suitable for additional person.
Price: Double $250. Single $150.
Meals: Full breakfast included.
Directions: Guest pick-up service from Nelson airport. From SH6 heading west from Nelson turn right onto SH60 heading for Collingwood. Take a left from the main highway onto Redwood Rd opposite the turn-off to Rabbit Island (also Redwood Rd). Stafford Place is 900m on the right, then 500m down a tree-lined drive.

Villa 10 Waterfront Apartments

Jenny Burton and Graham Snadden
10 Richardson Street, Nelson
Tel: 03-548-4619 Fax: 03-545-6110
Email: info@villa10.co.nz Web: www.villa10.co.nz
Cell: 027-601-6137

A very chirpy Jenny waving from the gate was not the only vibrant presence that greeted me on my arrival at Villa 10. On introduction to 'the loft' I was amazed by just how much sunshine you can fit into one room. Bright, cheeky blues and turquoises are brought to life with Jenny-designed cushions, sofa covers and curtains. The four-poster, a sheer masterpiece with regal curtained sides, deserves to be displayed in a gallery. Jenny is one of Nelson's many acclaimed artists and, although she no longer paints for a living, you are welcome to visit her downstairs studio where art has become an adventurous pleasure. Graham, meanwhile, is probably happier outside. A builder by trade, keen tramper and mountain biker, he knows the best local spots and will happily take you there. Together they architecturally redesigned and renovated this 1908 gem. The West Wing apartment retains a traditional feel with an open log fire and homely primary-coloured kitchen, which will bring any meal to life. I was astounded by the size of an ancient wisteria that had twined itself around the balcony. Villa 10's two very different apartments both share soaring views from their verandahs across Tasman Bay to the mountains of Kahurangi National Park. This peaceful hillside property is a perfect launch pad for Nelson restaurants and activities and the abundance of local wilderness.

Rooms: 2 self-contained apartments: 'The Loft' with 1 superking with en/s shower. 'The West Wing' with 1 queen, 1 twin and shared b/room. Both with full kitchen, lounge and laundry facilities.
Price: $255 each night, for first three nights. Then $10 less each extra night until $215. Min 2-night stay. Weekly and off-season rates available.
Meals: Fully self-catering. Breakfast provisions provided and starter-pack for week-long stays.
Directions: Heading out of Nelson on Rocks Road take the second turning on the left (Richardson Street) after The Boatshed restaurant.

Map Number: 4

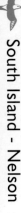

Te Puna Wai

Richard Hewetson and James Taylor
24 Richardson Street, Britannia Heights, Nelson
Tel: 03-548-7621 Fax: 03-548-7645
Email: stay@tepunawai.co.nz Web: www.tepunawai.co.nz
Cell: 021-679-795

The wide, open windows and verandahs at Te Puna Wai boast one of the best views in this book, straight out over Haulashore Island and the Nelson harbour entrance, with the Tasman and Arthur ranges to left and right respectively. The house is Richard and James's pride and joy, a mid-Victorian (1857) villa with a fine, intricate façade, the whole building restored and painstakingly completed under Richard's generalship. Guests have a choice of three rooms. Downstairs the Haulashore apartment has its own balcony, bedroom and state-of-the-art kitchen (chrome and granite grey) and a gorgeously green, marble-tiled bathroom with underfloor heating; the Wakatu room at the back also has a marble bathroom and the two rooms make a wonderful apartment for families. Or there's the attic Fifeshire suite, my personal favourite for its open wall of a window looking down at the bay and up at the stars. Arabian Nights notions leap to the imagination. The luxurious marble-tiled bathroom is full of whimsical design touches and has a wonderful full-length, claw-foot bath. There is a first-floor sitting-room with blue sofas, mango walls and wooden floors, many books and a stunning verandah with a low parapet. Richard is a truly talented linguist (German, French, Spanish and Portuguese) and much travelled. He and partner James provide a stylish, visually energising city retreat. Te Puna Wai must be one of the happiest places I have visited. Friendly cat in residence and many canine visitors. *High-speed Internet, guest PC.*

Rooms: 3: 1 self-contained apartment with queen, kitchen & en/s sh'r; 1 queen room with en/s shower (can be part of apartment); 1 suite: queen room, plus ante-room with double & full en/s bathroom.
Price: $195 for side room B&B, $295 for attic room B&B, $325 for apartment, $480 for downstairs double rooms let as one-party booking. Single, long-term & off-season rates available.
Meals: Complimentary drinks & full breakfast included. Guests in apartment can choose B&B or self-prepare breakfasts (provisions provided so not self-catering).
Directions: Map on Te Puna Wai web site.

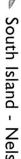

Retiro Park Lodge

Robbert de Jongh and Victor Flores

152 Teal Valley, Nelson
Tel: 03-545-0118
Email: info@retiroparklodge.co.nz Web: www.retiroparklodge.co.nz

Retiro Park Lodge certainly does justice to the picturesque central park in Madrid after which it was named. Many a walking track wind their way around the petite vineyard, olive and almond groves of the 50-acre farm. Donkeys, llamas and alpacas (all named according to the year in which they were born) will befriend you if you feed them and I'm sure that Flavia, a sleek, bouncy greyhound with the enthusiasm of a puppy, will accompany you on walks if you let her. Robbert has lived for over 20 years in Spain and has the collector gene. You'll find objects from all over the world that capture the attention and imagination. A vast opulent bathroom in the main house echoes the Mediterranean in vivid terracotta and deep blues, while the impressive barn conversion is fresh and light and allows for a little more independence. Robbert and Victor encourage guests to dine with them on their first night, and I certainly had a fantastic time shooting the breeze with them over a leisurely meal. The couple share a sharp sense of humour and an enthusiasm for the world that will keep you chatting for hours. Since Victor is a trained chef I can assure you that both food and company will be wonderful, and I will be sorely jealous. The lodge is only 15 minutes from Nelson with its numerous galleries, restaurants and activities. But Retiro's Spanish translation is 'retreat' and I would take the hint. *Your hosts speak English, Spanish and Dutch. Tours of Abel-Tasman can be arranged through here. Wireless broadband.*

Rooms: 2: 1 queen with en-suite bathroom in the lodge and 1 queen with en-suite bathroom and kitchenette in converted barn. Additional single room in lodge and day bed in barn available on request.
Price: $250 - $275. Singles $150.
Meals: Full breakfast included. Picnic lunches and 3-course dinner available by arrangement, both at additional cost. Dinner $150 (wine inc). Can be self-catering.
Directions: From Nelson travel 14km on SH 6 towards Blenheim. Turn R into Teal Valley Rd and travel a further 1.4km to private road. Retiro Park Lodge is signed on the right 200m on.

Map Number: 4

Jefferswood

Jeff and Sandra Sewell

Jefferswood, Camerons Road, RD1, Havelock
Tel: 03-572-8081 Fax: 03-572-8091
Email: info@jefferswood.co.nz Web: www.jefferswood.co.nz

Not a slap of paint or a scrap of wallpaper tarnish this wheat-coloured mud-brick treasure; there's just thought-provoking art hanging on walls that breathe with the conditions, keeping cool in the summer and warm in the winter… why aren't all places this logical? Not only ideal for humankind… Mother Nature is also a big fan of Jefferswood: I counted eight tuis zipping about the garden, in and out of the flowering cherries and the bird-rich crab-apples. The organic garden pumps out produce and the orchard dishes up plums, apples, nectarines, apricots and hazelnuts. Combine this with home-made yoghurt, bread and muesli, and you will be the only thing that is spoilt rotten at breakfast! The evening meal is up to you: try picking a salad from Sandra's garden and doing dinner Kiwi-style at the barbecue, under the shaded canopy of the 350-year-old totara. Enjoy a crisp Marlborough sauvignon blanc and that summer sizzling sound harmonising with the bell-birds. I seemed to see, taste and hear better here and really noticed the details; perhaps it's because this is the first place I've visited where the commercial distortion of TV has been bravely rejected for more traditional, communicative and relaxing pastimes: conversation, music, books, big leather couches, studying the night's crystal-clear constellations and taking rides in Jeff's 1965 MGB Roadster. In short, this is the place to shut out the hubbub of the modern world and enjoy some good natural living.

Rooms: 2: 1 superking and 1 queen, both with en-suite showers.
Price: $295 - $325.
Meals: Full breakfast and complimentry wine, tea and coffee with home baking. BBQ available for self-catering.
Directions: From Blenheim take SH6 through Renwick continuing towards Havelock. Look for Camerons Road on your L. From Nelson go through Havelock (if coming along Queen Charlotte Drive from Picton, turn L at the SH6 turn-off). Look for Camerons Road on your R. Jefferswood is 300m down Camerons Road.

Mudbrick Lodge

Tania Lawrence
Rimu Gully, Rai Valley
Tel: 03-571-6147 Fax: 03-571-6147
Email: tania@mudbricklodge.co.nz Web: www.mudbricklodge.co.nz
Cell: 027-251-3867

A genuine country retreat that swarms with animals, Mudbrick Lodge is blissfully cut off and blissfully quiet – the kind of place that we feel rather guilty about sharing with the world. Kelvin is a man of the land and can take you on true-blue hunting trips, while Tania is young, enthusiastic and a trained chef. This last fact you must be sure to take advantage of. She serves breakfast in the main house in a conservatory overlooking the 1,000-acre valley. Along with the resident dog and cats, I gravitated towards the kitchen (complete with coffee-machine – Tania is an Auckland escapee after all), where we chatted over mountains of food. The bedrooms in the separate guest cottage are lovely with huge beds. In my wood-burner-warmed room, there was a double shower complete with Morris and James tiles depicting local bird life and a brand-new kitchenette is planned for readiness by the time we go to print. The lodge is made of mud bricks (a combination of mud, sand and straw), which keep the rooms warm even in the coldest weather – something this weedy Brit much appreciated. A new spa pool has just been added and Tania, and Kelvin, have just planted a 1.5 acre truffieres, due to produce in 2011. I love it here. It feels like staying with an old friend.

Rooms: 2: both semi-self-contained deluxe suites with superking/twin and en/s shower. 1 has double shower.
Price: $220 - $260. Singles on application.
Meals: Full breakfast included. Dinners $50 p.p. Full wine list available. Packed lunches $20 p.p.
Directions: From Blenheim take SH6 towards Nelson. In Rai Valley turn right just after the shops (signposted French Pass). Over the bridge, turn right and then right again. Then turn left which becomes unsealed road and lodge is at the end.

Map Number: 4

Entry Number: 52

Cove Cottage

Sue and Nigel Hutchinson

Jetty 45, Double Cove, Picton
Tel: 03-573-4153
Email: doublecove@xtra.co.nz Web: www.doublecove.co.nz
Cell: 021-433-921

It's not everywhere you can go for a daybreak stroll in your pyjamas without fear of embarrassment, but at Cove Cottage that is exactly what I did. Lazily reclining on the second peninsula of Double Cove this unpretentious bach trails its gaze through blue topaz waters on both sides. Wedged between a rising backdrop of private woodland and the sea, this 'boat-access-only' spot is an entirely secluded resort in itself. Between much laughter and stories of Land Rover adventures through Africa, Kiwi-Sue and Brit-Nigel told me of quirky Cove Cottage's development from its humble origins as a ramshackle shed. Wonderfully friendly and fascinating people, they have injected the cottage with a full dose of character. The marine motif is subtle and interesting: driftwood-framed mirror, old shell-shaded lights on pulley systems, flags and lighthouses. Also the 'sleep out,' a romantic hideaway with its own en-suite bathroom just up the path, is great for couples (although the beds can be twins if required). You won't be watching the TV with kayaks, rowing-boats, walks and art materials to play with, but you could always pop on 'Goodbye Porkpie' which was produced by your host! The deck next to the dock takes full advantage of a BBQ-friendly sunspot. Here I imagine many a sunset sinking into the night carried on a wave of fun, food... and probably booze. Private walking tracks in hills around the bay and a link to the Queen Charlotte track walk (perhaps accompanied by friendly lab Fraser) and dolphin-watching trips are arranged as well as tours to bird and animal sanctuaries.

Rooms: 1 self-catering cottage: 1 double room with king-size bed and 1 twin room with shared shower. Additional king/twin with e/s shower in the 'cabin'.
Price: From $250 - $350 for first couple per night. $60 for each additional person.
Meals: Fully self-catering. BBQ facilities and gas supplied. Can pre-arrange cupboards to be stocked beforehand with basic supplies, provided list sent at time of booking.
Directions: 4km from Picton. Boat access only. Details of water taxis operating from Picton will be emailed on confirmation.

Straw Lodge

Nettie Barrow and Jane Craighead

17 Fareham Lane, Blenheim
Tel: 03-572-9767 Fax: 03-572-9769
Email: strawlodge@xtra.co.nz Web: www.strawlodge.co.nz

What a cheery place! I defy any of you to leave Straw Lodge without a spring in your step. Interesting, super-friendly hosts, lots of wine, good food and charming accommodation constructed of straw and plastered to create an atmospheric, well-insulated, rustic walling. Eight years ago this area was just paddocks, but now 19 acres of vines reach virtually to the doors of the guest rooms in this picture-postcard setting in the Wairau Valley. The surroundings are ideal for sitting back, ordering one of Nettie and Jane's hearty vineyard platters, or firing up the barbecue, and indulging in a few 'in-house' sauvignon blancs or pinot noirs, made by a local wine-maker from Straw Lodge grapes. In warm weather (virtually the whole year in sunny Blenheim) meals are served outside on a long table under trellises, a setting that reminded me of those country feast scenes from olive oil adverts. Guests stay in vineyard suites either side of the main house, but you're welcome, nay expected, to roam unfettered. There's a woody lounge with big beams and a large fire, a spa under the stars, private courtyards and BBQ areas, plus DVDs, CDs and TVs in all the rooms. Needless to say, it was definitely a wrench to leave. Nettie and Jane advise you about all sorts of wine-tasting, walking, 4X4, fishing and cycling excursions. *Complimentary golf clubs, mountain and electric bikes, and wine-tasting available for guests.*

Rooms: 3: 2 Vineyard Suites, with king/twin + double sofa-bed, and 1 queen suite. All have en-suite showers.
Price: $295 - $395. Singles $265 - $365. Extra person $90. Child (under 12) $60. Single night booking surcharge $50.
Meals: Full gourmet cooked breakfast included. Complimentary wine tasting. Substantial vineyard platters for 2 $75. Self-catering available, plus BBQ alfresco dining area for guest use.
Directions: From Blenheim, head towards Nelson on SH6, then turn left onto SH63 towards the west coast. Travel for just over 7km to Fareham Lane on your right. The house is 200m down here.

Map Number: 3 & 4

Entry Number: 54

Brancott Ridge

Margaret and Peter Foster

Brancott Ridge, 226 Wrekin Road, Blenheim
Tel: 03-572-9140
Email: stay@brancottridge.co.nz Web: www.brancottridge.co.nz
Cell: 021-614-696

UK-born Peter and Margaret settled here after circumnavigating the South Island on bikes and discovering idyllic Blenheim. Here Brancott Ridge overlooks square miles of some of New Zealand's finest vineyards, then Cloudy Bay, then the Cook Strait and onward, to the mighty shadow of the North Island floating on the horizon. The elongated house sits harmoniously within the raw beauty of Blenheim's foothills and on a summer's evening, I suggest you pick up a pizza, a bottle of wine and wander to the private lookout. As the temperature recedes you can watch the valley flood with warm pastel shades, hazing the landscape into an impressionist vision. Come dark, the telescope's there to explore the star-dusted canopy. Inside you'll find a modern house with antiques and historical memorabilia: an original 1790 map of Captain Cook's 1770 New Zealand voyage; a 1590 solid English oak Armada chest; a 1760 grandfather clock; and liquor flasks with a story to fire the imagination. I can't forget the beds. They're from Denmark (by royal appointment no less) and incredibly comfortable. When you wake, the swamp kauri dining table carries a plentiful breakfast that will make lunch irrelevant, so you've time to play with Tilly, the little fox terrier. She may be tied up when you arrive… Let her off and she'll be your friend for life.

Rooms: 2: both with superkings (1 converts to twin) with large en/s showers.
Price: $380. Minimum two-night stay.
Meals: Full breakfast provided with a variety of cooked options available including a gourmet bacon sandwich, croissants, traditional English, or a three-egg omelette.
Directions: From Blenheim, it's a 15 minute drive including a 2 km unsealed driveway. From Blenheim, take SH63 towards Nelson. Turn left at Bells Road. Then right at New Renwick Road. Left at Brancott Road. Right at Wrekin Road where Brancott Ridge is sign-posted at the end.

Entry Number: 55

Map Number: 3 & 4

Cob Quarters

Jenny and Roland Mapp

Spray Point Station, 4540 Waihopai Valley Road, RD 6 Blenheim
Tel: 03-572-4222
Email: info@spraypoint.co.nz Web: www.spraypoint.co.nz

The majority of the cob cottages that once peppered the historic Marlborough drover's route have since crumbled, but Spray Point Station stands prouder than ever. Shepherds are not the only ones who have sheltered here over the past century. Generations of birds, possums and occasional cows that have almost licked the walls down have enjoyed the abandoned years. The Mapps found it in a sickly state, but breathed new life into its mud walls to preserve its rustic charm: drover graffiti is still pencilled onto the walls and the original open fire still burns bright; the intricate swallows' nests still ornament the corners and old dynamite boxes act as side tables; the lanterns remain too, but with the luxury of electricity burning within. The experience truly amplifies when you use the idyllic open-air shower; continuous hot water rains from a hillside overlooking the swimming-hole-sprinkled Waihopai River. The two open-air, cast-iron baths have the same view. There's also a barbecue, but Jenny is happy to whip up some high-country fare in your honour. I suggest you work up an appetite first by exploring the station. This is trekking country, so aim for the rewarding summit views of this isolated land inhabited by wild deer, pigs, goats, chamois, kingfishers, plovers and native falcons. This is one of the more treasured places I've ever stayed. Book a couple of nights here and you're really living.

Rooms: 1 self-contained cottage with queen and 4 extra sized bunks. Separate bathroom & outside shower. Limited numbers. Bookings essential.
Price: $200 - $220 per couple per night depending on season & public holidays & $30 per extra person.
Meals: Home-made 2-course meal $30 pp & $20 per bottle of good-quality local wine. Catered picnic meals also available by arrangement.
Directions: From Blenheim take State Highway 63 until reach Waihopai Valley Rd turn-off. Then drive 45km, last few kms on gravel rd. Look for big Cob Quarters sign which is the driveway after 4540 Spray Point Station.

Map Number: 4

Entry Number: 56

Austin Heights Boutique Bed and Breakfast

John and Lynne McGinn

19 Austin Street, On the Peninsula, Kaikoura
Tel: 03-319-5836 Fax: 03-319-6836
Email: austinheights@xtra.co.nz Web: www.austinheights.co.nz
Cell: 021-295-7031

Austin Heights sits above Kaikoura and commands sumptuous views down to the sea and across to the (often) snow-capped mountains. When I visited the beautiful garden was brightly ablaze in the chilly autumn sunshine, so I was content to retreat into warmer quarters. The guest units with their two big bedrooms are situated above the McGinns' home. They have small kitchens with myriad teas and coffees, bowls of fresh fruit, plus chocolates and biscuits for the middle of the night. And, for those brief hours when you're not charging around Kaikoura whale-watching, dolphin-watching, wine-tasting and sightseeing, a stereo, DVD player (plus movies) and 32-inch flat-screen digital satellite TV's in both upstairs suites are your friends should you have need of them. The rooms are connected to the main house by a long balcony where you can sit and applaud quietly as the sun sets gently over the hills. John and Lynne can proudly claim all credit for the transformation of Austin Heights (including the outdoor hydrotherapy spa) some few years ago. Now dab hands in B&B they serve breakfast and advice in the main house at a long wooden table. This is a comfortable seaside base for exploring the area's considerable charms and just a five-minute walk to the sea. It would make an excellent stopping point for two couples travelling together as you can make it into your own private apartment. Gentle giant of a cat, answering to 'Oscar', in situ. *Free pick-up service from bus or train. Handy to all major amenities. 10 mins' walk to the sea.*

Rooms: 3 apartments: 1 queen suite with en/s shower; 1 family apartment downstairs with shower and bath, 1 double & 1 single bed plus a 3/4 sofa bed; 1 superking suite.
Price: $195 - $265.
Meals: Generous continental breakfast included. Cooked available. Several good restaurants in the area.
Directions: Heading south from the centre of Kaikoura (signposted Christchurch) turn left into Scarborough Street and keep going until you get to Austin Street which is the 2nd turning on your left.

Charwell Lodge

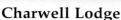

Bill and Judy Clarkson
82 Medway Road, Hanmer Springs
Tel: 03-315-5070 Fax: 03-315-5071
Email: william.clarkson@xtra.co.nz Web: www.charwell.co.nz
Cell: 021-347-905

With uncanny timing, I arrived at what could have been an awkward moment as the lodge was full of Bill and Judy's friends who had all popped in after a big get-together in the mountains the previous day. But we all got nattering so easily that I would have wanted to include Charwell even if the rooms had resembled medieval penitentiary cells. Unsurprisingly, the bedrooms were all wonderful with top-class linens, throws and curtains made by Judy and serene private verandahs with views over the southern mountains. And these views are mesmerising, across the spread of the plains below with the broad Waiau River curling through, and (on my visit) the snow-topped mountains across the valley wreathed in mist. Relax in the jacuzzi and relish the perfection. The house was built in country style with old doors salvaged from demolition yards. The rimu front door (complete with iron horse's head bell), for example, came from a girls' school in Christchurch. There are a lot of African and South American artefacts from the couple's time abroad and a David Shepherd painting in the guest living room that Bill carried rolled up in his rucksack for months on end during their travels. I met Charlotte the goat and completely lost track of time. Don't make the same mistake as I did and have to leave too soon. *Hanmer Hot Springs five minutes down the road. Closed 25th December.*

Rooms: 3: 1 king with en/s bath and shower; 1 queen with en/s shower; 1 superking/twin with en/s shower.
Price: $198 - $240. Singles $198. Enquire about winter specials. 'Pamper packages' available.
Meals: Full breakfast included. Packed lunches possible for day trips out. Dinners by arrangement. Complimentary glass of wine at 6pm.
Directions: From SH7 turn right into SH7A (signposted Hanmer Springs). Cross the ferry bridge and take the next right into Medway Road where the lodge is signposted.

Amuri Estate and Retreat

Lisa and Chris Preston
128 Medway Road, Hamner Springs
Tel: 03-315-5059
Email: info@amuri.co.nz Web: www.amuri.co.nz
Cell: 0274-582-886

Amuri means 'land of the shining tussock', named after the wind that ripples over the Hanmer basin grasslands like water. Such romantic imagery can be admired from the estate's mesmerising view of Hanmer's moody plains, which slowly change colour throughout the day, only slumbering into darkness when the evening lights of the town are illuminated under the distant Hanmer Range. I strolled over this subdivision that was once just pasture, taking note of how Chris and Lisa's decade of hard work was now paying off. The 1,300 trees are producing high-quality extra virgin olive oil and the new lodge is open for guests. The lounge is comfortably furnished with captivating chairs, a gas fire and double doors that open onto a deck that runs along the wing of large rooms. Each suite is blessed with the same wide and wonderful view and also many luxuries such as Egyptian cotton linen, wool rests, Fairydown quilts and DVD players with which to indulge in a great movie and music collection available for guests. Hunger will probably motivate a hilly ten-minute amble from the schist entrance to the nearby first-class restaurant; but you may prefer to stay in after Amuri's 'A Taste of Italy'. This involves an extensive run-down on New Zealand's olive oil industry at two-hour public tastings, along with antipasto platters, local wine and a flavour of the oil pressed from olives plucked from Amuri Estate's trees. Amuri's a treat and the perfect welcome to Hanmer Springs.

Rooms: 3 rooms and 1 cottage: 1 king with en/s shower, 1 king/twin with en/s shower, 1 super king with en/s shower and spa bath. Cottage is self-contained with king and en/s shower.
Price: $200 - $350.
Meals: Full breakfast, pre-dinner drink and canapés included. 'Taste of Italy' enquiries welcome.
Directions: Taking SH 7a towards Hanmer Springs, cross the single lane bridge across the Waiau River gorge, take Medway Road on your right, before the Hanmer River bridge. Go 2km, you'll see two stone pillars on the right; head up this drive and 'Amuri Estate Retreat' is signposted on the left.

Okuku Country Estate

Lorraine and Robert Smith

2 Rakahuri Road, Rangiora, North Canterbury
Tel: 03-312-8740 Fax: 03-312-8122
Email: enquiries@okukucountryestate.co.nz
Web: www.okukucountryestate.co.nz

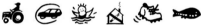

Even the driveway is special at Okuku, winding through fields of freshly-cut hay and a tall grove of trees before arriving at the entrance of this beautiful, Italian Renaissance-influenced homestead. The interior is every bit as grand as the exterior: original artworks, antique furniture, middle-eastern carpets; floorboards characteristically pitted from decades of dancing stilettos; a classic billiard room and an impressively large indoor pool; and immense fireplaces, two of which still shelter open flames throughout winter months. Lorraine has elegantly decorated the bedrooms, like the Wong Room, a gentlemanly space that once belonged to the head servant (I sort of expected there must be a White Room somewhere too); or the Rose Room, more suited to ladies with its petite writing desk; or the smaller Daffodil room, best in spring when its sash-windowed view over 10,000 daffodils comes into its own. The daffs grow within four acres of manicured garden, cedars, elms, oaks, beeches, redwoods and a variety of orchard trees. It's pleasantly isolated from the tourist trail here, but there's still plenty to do: Mount Thomas National Park, Woodland Beach, Jo Seeger's reputable restaurant and Pegasus Bay Vineyard are all short drives away. You're only 40 minutes from Mount Hutt's ski fields and the Ashley River borders the property, if you fancy fly-fishing. But there's no need to stray far, especially with such friendly hosts, home-made baking, afternoon tea, apéritifs and an elegant three-course dinner in picture-book surroundings all included in the experience.

Rooms: 6: 1 with king and single; 2 with kings; and 3 with queens. All en/s showers. Only three separate groups can stay at one time.

Price: $450 - $500. Singles $300.

Meals: A great dining experience all included in the tariff: full breakfast, afternoon tea with homemade baking, pre-dinner drinks, 3 course evening meal with bottle of wine.

Directions: From Christchurch drive to Rangiora then follow road to Loburn. Turn L into Hodgsons Road (Okuku Country Estate is AA signed here). Drive 18km to go over Garry River Bridge, then L into Rakahuri Rd. Full directions on Okuku web site.

Map Number: 4

Entry Number: 60

Clearview Lodge

Robin and Sue Clements

8 Clearwater Avenue, Harewood, Christchurch
Tel: 03-359-5797 Fax: 03-358-9131
Email: relax@clearviewlodge.com Web: www.clearviewlodge.com
Cell: 021-727-883

I was so overwhelmed by the presence of Clearview Lodge as I approached that I initially failed to notice the fully-fledged orchard and olive groves that were passing by. It may only be about ten minutes from the airport, but you could be halfway up Everest such is the spirit of peace and quiet here. Set in ten acres of vineyards and pure greenery, the lodge was built by Sue and Robin seven years ago with future guests in mind. Bedrooms are therefore large and luxurious – mine had deep red walls, antique chairs, a TV (with Sky, if it matters), Wifi and copious amounts of fruit and chocs. The bathrooms are, if anything, even bigger. From my balcony I could gaze freely across Sue's wild garden (with essential herb and veggie area) and out to the vines. It's a siren for local bird life, including a family of quails who surveyed me from the front lawn as I made my way towards the first meal of the day. Breakfast is an almost horizontally laid-back affair, taken at a table in front of long windows with yet more views over the grounds. Their cellar is well stocked with wines produced from their own vines (2006 from "best ever seen" grapes is still the pick of the vintages... but going fast) so I suggest you grab a glass or three and lie back in the spa pool – a perfect way to recover from any long and arduous flight. *Championship golf course and The Groynes just down the road. Also fully kitted-out and great for kids. Heated outdoor pool.*

Rooms: 3: all superking/twins, 2 with en/s bath and shower; 1 with en/s shower.
Price: $325 - $375.
Meals: Full breakfast included.
Directions: From airport turn left at the 2nd roundabout onto Russley Road (SH1). After 4km (becomes Johns Road) turn left into Clearwater Avenue and the lodge is the first driveway on the right.

Historic Hambledon

Brent and Claire Smith
103 Bealey Avenue, Christchurch
Tel: 03-379-0723 Fax: 03-379-0758
Email: stay@hambledon.co.nz Web: www.hambledon.co.nz

My first-ever night in New Zealand was spent at Hambledon, raising the bar very high for those that followed. Brent and Claire are proud of their magnificent, many-roofed 1856 home, which thrills with its colourful walls and beautiful wood panelling. Hearts and wallets have gone into the restoration and conversion of this mansion back from a series of apartments to the unified building it once was and creating extensive cottage gardens. One big change from the house of yore though: imposing Victorian mansions were not meant to be this comfortable. I genuinely couldn't wait for bed (sad, I know). I was sleeping in an antique half-tester awash with luxurious duvet, white cotton and soft gold curtains. Beside me a red carpet sidled up to pale green walls and big windows, and a door led to a separate kitchen area and perky yellow shower room. The other spacious rooms were equally fine, some with four-posters, and all mixed antiques with many modern extras like hair-dryers, bathrobes, TVs, videos, phones and fridges. The house is very central; only five minutes walk to Hagley Park and ten to town, so leave the car in the driveway. Breakfast was a you-won't-need-lunch extravaganza – six cereals, five dried fruits or nuts, two stewed fruits, yoghurt, raisin bread, fresh croissants and French toast with maple syrup, banana and bacon. I'm still digesting happily.

Rooms: 4 suites: 1 king/single, 1 queen/single, 1 x 2-bedroom king/twin, 1 x 2-bedroom queen/twin. All with en/s shower.
Price: $250 - $380. Longer-term self-catering accommodation available.
Meals: Full breakfast included. Complimentary drinks offered. More than 15 good restaurants within walking distance.
Directions: From Hagley Park, continue up Bealey Ave. Historic Hambledon is just before Springfield Road.

Map Number: 4

The Weston House

Leonard and Stephanie May

62 Park Terrace, Christchurch
Tel: 03-366-0234 Fax: 03-366-5254
Email: enquiries@westonhouse.co.nz Web: www.westonhouse.co.nz

This imposing neo-Georgian house (built in 1922) sits slap-bang in the middle of Christchurch. Technically guests stay in the servants' quarters, but have no fear, this is no 'Upstairs, Downstairs' arrangement. Bedrooms are English in feel but immaculately turned out in a way that I can never manage at home. The whole house has been given a lavish makeover and I don't think I have ever seen rooms with so many extras. Hidden in cupboards are telephones, bathrobes, corkscrews, more toiletries than you can shake a stick at, fridges, your own heating system and mohair rugs... to name but a few. No one seems to have told Stephanie and Leonard that they are under no obligation to provide everything for their guests. When I arrived Stephanie was in mid-conversation with two guests and the sound of laughter filled the air (always a good sign). Drinks are taken on the front terrace to catch the last of the sun and vicious games of croquet are often played out on the vast front lawn. Breakfast is a moveable and memorable feast and Stephanie admits that she is particularly famous for her salmon and brie omelettes. Fresh flowers and home-baking complete the picture. This grand residence may stand in the most prestigious street in town, but it's a totally un-stuffy place to stay and lots of fun. Incredibly central and a five-minute walk to the centre of town. Wifi internet access throughout house (and garden!). Also a computer dedicated to guest use - Photoshop & Picasa loaded - and Stephanie says she will even copy your photos to a disc... for free!.

Rooms: 2: 1 superking/twin with en/s shower; 1 queen with private bathroom with shower (but you are on your own landing, next to the bathroom).
Price: $430. No single rates.
Meals: Full breakfast included. Complimentary drinks served at 6pm. Restaurants surround you! Picnic hampers can be provided.
Directions: Eastern boundary of Hagley Park, corner of Peterborough St and Park Terrace. Stephanie or Leonard are happy to pick you up or drop you off at the airport too by the way.

Onuku Bed and Breakfast

Jenny and Bob Wilkinson

27 Harry Ell Drive, Cashmere, Christchurch
Tel: 03-332-7296
Email: bob.wilkinson@paradise.net.nz Web: onukubedandbreakfast.co.nz
Cell: 027-2451-360

At Onuku I was made to feel instantly at home by Reggie, an energetic, very happy black labrador. By the time I was upstairs sitting comfortably with a glass of wine in my hand on a vast sofa overlooking the night lights of Christchurch I'd realised the cause of his good humour – life at Onuku for himself, for the Wilkinsons, and for their guests is really pretty good. If I'd had a tail it would have been wagging too. Designed by a celebrated local architect the long and stylish contemporary, open-plan sitting room boasts Persian rugs, native wood floors and floor-to-ceiling windows, which offer a view out over the city to the Southern Alps and Pegasus Bay. Plans for a roof garden are also under way. Jenny is a keen bridge player and will play with guests, but be warned: she has played for the NZ national team for 12 years. Bob, when he's not working as a tour guide in NZ and Australia, can take guests golfing, fishing and walking. He is an expert on local flora and fauna. Both love to cook and Jenny has a particular passion for Thai food. I can certainly vouch for her excellent Kiwi cuisine. Onuku is only 15 mins drive from central Christchurch, but is right on the edge of Victoria Park so there's peace, quiet and walks aplenty from the house.

Rooms: 3: 2 queens en/s with shower; 1 twin en/s with shower and adjoining sitting room.
Price: $100 - $175. Extra person $50. Singles on request. Shuttle from airport by arrangement.
Meals: Full breakfast included. Dinner by arrangement: $30.
Directions: Drive south towards hills & continue up either Dyers Pass or Hackthorne Rds for about 3km until reach crossroads & Takahe (large stone building). Continue up L on Victoria Pk Rd & turn L at Longhurst Terr. Travel along this terrace until Harry Ell Drive (3rd on R).

Map Number: 4

Ballymoney Farmstay and Garden

Merrilies Rebbeck
Wardstay Road, RD2, Christchurch
Tel: 03-329-6706 Fax: 03-329-6709
Email: info@ballymoney.co.nz Web: www.ballymoney.co.nz

Just a 20-minute drive from Christchurch airport I found myself out in the country where the Rebbeck family have been modifying their 100-year-old farmhouse and land for years, stripping back wood panelling, adding bits on, tending the two-acre garden and planting hundreds of trees. Merrilies has the arty genes; she's the mother of a painter and her daughters' artwork is exhibited on the walls. She also has a wonderful eye for interiors; the farmhouse feels earthy, homely and elegant, with wooden floors, kilims and seagrass matting. Merrilies wears many hats, farmer's and chef's among them; when I stayed we sat down to lamb, potatoes, kumara, leeks and chestnuts, all from the farm, rounded off with home-made apple sorbet with Galliano. After breakfast I was whisked around the property on a 4-wheel motorbike to admire Dexter cattle, Dorset horned sheep, saddle-back pigs, white peacocks, black and white ducks, hens... and a sly donkey who is a bit of an escape artist and known to take himself for a stroll to the distant property boundary. If you go looking for him, I suggest you also take a detour through the garden and orchard to the pond full of bird-life. When you get back, rest those sore muscles in the outdoor hot tub, set on a platform with views over the garden. Or just relax inside. In either case, Ballymoney is lots of fun.

Rooms: 2: Manuka Suite has king/twin with en-suite shower plus extra queen room with private bath and shower; Kowhai Studio with 1 queen and 1 single with en/s shower.
Price: $200 - $270. Singles $170.
Meals: Full breakfast included. Dinners $50 pp for 2 courses including wine. Kids eat free between 5pm and 6pm.
Directions: From Christchurch take SH75 to Tai Tapu. Turn right towards Lincoln. After 2km turn left into Wardstay Rd. Travel 800m to Ballymoney on right.

Kawatea Farmstay

Judy and Kerry Thacker
1048 Okains Bay Rd, Akaroa RD 3, Banks Peninsula
Tel: 03-304-8621 Fax: 03-304-8621
Email: kawatea@xtra.co.nz Web: www.kawateafarmstay.co.nz

The drive into the Banks Peninsula was a great way to start my New Zealand tour, chugging along the edges of volcanic highlands that plummet into the sea inlets far below and then curling down the steep hillside roads to isolated farming communities such as Okains Bay. Kawatea is surrounded by a high collar of green hills dotted with grazing cattle and Thacker territory stretches through 1,400 acres of dramatic scenery, which perhaps is wasted on the cattle, but not on you. Guests can take picnics out on foot to the Heads and safe, sandy, swimming beaches, and walking in the hills is peerless. Back at the 100-year-old homestead all is superbly comfortable, with carved fireplaces, deep sofas, high ceilings, wooden floors and rugs, each room huge with its own deck, views of the hills, the nearby flower garden, the sea. There are pet lambs in spring and a field of tame sheep to feed right by the house. This is a proper farm and you eat *en famille* (beef, lamb, fish, fruit and veg mostly home-grown), breakfast in the sunny conservatory. *Kayaks available. Trips to seals, dolphins, penguins can be arranged. The peninsula rewards stays of longer than one night!*

Rooms: 3: 1 queen and king-single with en/s shower; 1 queen with private bathroom with bath, shower and separate toilet. Also 1 queen and single with shared bathroom available if family or group booking.
Price: $125 - $155. Singles $85 – $155.
Meals: Full breakfast included. Dinner by arrangement: $35 - $40 pp.
Directions: From Christchurch follow highway 75km signed to Akaroa. 2km past Duvauchelle turn left, signed Okains Bay Road. 11km to the house.

Map Number: 4

Entry Number: 66

Maison de la Mer

Carol and Bruce Hyland

1 Rue Benoit, Akaroa
Tel: 03-304-8907 Fax: 03-304-8917
Email: maisondelamer@xtra.co.nz Web: www.maisondelamer.co.nz
Cell: 021-986-221

As we sat chatting on the sunny verandah, I listened with a landlubber's awe to Carol and Bruce's swashbuckling tales of adventures on the high seas. Well… three years spent living on yachts, sailing their family from Bruce's native Canada, down to the Caribbean and back. The house is as inspiring as its owners – my editor claimed their last incarnation, a B&B in Auckland, should have been "set on a pedestal and paraded around the world". Well, they've only done it again! Maison de la Mer is a truly wonderful house, full of antique furniture, Persian carpets and contemporary art. The bedrooms have individual styles, but all share under-floor heating, stunning views across the harbour, honesty bars, masses of fresh flowers, home-made shortbread and complimentary port (I particularly liked the nautically-themed Boathouse). Akaroa was originally a French whaling port and they must have left behind a few good recipes as the town now boasts three of the country's finest restaurants, all within easy walking distance of Maison de la Mer. However, in the morning Carol, Bruce and their phenomenal breakfasts are very hard to beat. You should be keel-hauled or at least made to walk a plank if you don't find time to stay here. *Bush walks, penguins, fur seals and swimming with dolphins all available nearby.*

Rooms: 3: 2 kings, 1 queen, 2 with en/s shower, 1 with en/s shower and spa bath.
Price: $400 - $450.
Meals: Full breakfast included.
Directions: From Christchurch, highway 75 to the centre of Akaroa, past the Post Office, on the corner of Rue Lavaud and Rue Benoit, on your left.

Onuku Heights

Eckhard Keppler

166 Haylocks Road, Akaroa
Tel: 03-304-7112 Fax: 03-304-7116
Email: onuku.heights@paradise.net.nz Web: www.onuku-heights.co.nz

I had been told to expect great views in New Zealand and was determined not to be too easily impressed. Yet this carefully prepared insouciance counted for nothing when I reached Onuku Heights. My range of exclamations was found wanting. You approach the isolated 1860s farmhouse up a winding gravel road that crosses several small streams. It's the highest property for miles, perched on the side of a hill. From the terrace at the front, home of a beautiful, heated and beautifully-located swimming pool, the ground drops steeply away, sending the eye tumbling through vistas of pastures and trees to the turquoise blue of Akaroa Harbour and on to the hills beyond. You're engulfed by nature, with a grove of enormous macrocarpa and 100-year-old totara, matai and beech in a 50-acre reserve. Then there are camellias, proteas, lillies, roses and a small orchard (supplying much of the breakfast fruit). When not sheep farming, Eckhard has found time to restore the house: the bedrooms are great, floored with rimu and furnished with antiques and expensive beds and there's an open fire in the guest lounge. Two rooms in the house look over that view, but there is also a separate, larger cottage room, looking to the rose garden. All breathtaking stuff and you're just 15 minutes from Akaroa. *More great views from walking tracks (1 hour to 1 day) stretching over the 800-acre property. Heated swimming pool and sauna. Horse trekking available. Privately-guided rides on well-mannered Quarter Horses.*

Rooms: 3: all kings with en-suite shower.
Price: $240 - $350.
Meals: Full breakfast included.
Directions: Turn left at the southern end of Akaroa (at the bakery) onto Rue Jolie. Follow signs to Onuku Marae. After the Marae, continue into Haylocks Rd and farm is at the end.

Matuka Lodge

Rosalie and Russell Smith
395 Glen Lyon Rd, Twizel
Tel: 03-435-0144
Email: info@matukalodge.co.nz Web: www.matukalodge.co.nz
Cell: 027-426-1213

As I crested a hill all that lay before me - the strange turquoise surfaces of Lakes Pukaki and Tekapo and the magnificence of Mt Cook - radiated an ethereal, almost surreal beauty as they shimmered in the pure sunshine. I had to stop and stare for quite some time. Eventually, following the blue canals, I made my way to Matuka Lodge, which imitates the iconic Kiwi shed with corrugated iron protecting its symmetrical shoulders, and which revels in its own private slice of this extraordinary landscape. Rosalie welcomed me in and before long I was sitting down to a hot cuppa in the lounge, making appreciative mental notes of all the eye-arresting original art works gathered by the Smiths during their years in South Africa and Australia. This place is a real home and I felt very welcome. The den's bookshelf spills over with paperbacks and the kitchen has a variety of gourmet teas, good coffee and wines and beers whenever you want them. The restful suites all pay due homage to the wondrous views, particularly the premiere rooms where you can watch, from the luxury of a double spa bath, the preternatural colours of the landscape slowly kaleidoscope one to another as the sun heads west. Nearer to home the rooms look out onto a trout- and lily-filled lake. Rosalie assures me that the trout glide undisturbed by line or lure, even though Russell is a passionate fly-fisherman. Instead he heads for other local rivers in this gateway to Mount Cook, surely one of the most spectacular gateways to anywhere on earth. Matuka Lodge fits right in.

Rooms: 4: 2 kings with en/s shower; 2 superking/twins with en/s shower and spa bath.
Price: Kings: single night $465; 2 or more nights $425. Superkings: single night $535; 2 or more nights $495.
Meals: Full breakfast and complimentary pre-dinner drink included. Happy to recommend restaurants.
Directions: From north: 8km after turn-off to Aoraki/Mt Cook, cross the Twizel River and take next right, Glen Lyon Road. From south: 30km after Omarama, pass both Twizel turn-offs, take the next left, Glen Lyon Road. 4km from highway turn left into Old Station Road. Matuka Lodge is on your left.

Twin Peaks

Margaret and Derek Bulman

661 Frankton Rd, Queenstown
Tel: 03-441-8442 Fax: 03-441-8575
Email: bulman@twinpeaks.co.nz Web: www.twinpeaks.co.nz
Cell: 021-685-520

Do the bedrooms have walls? Is the lake in the sitting-room? Twin Peaks is a stunning modern design with a glassed-in cloister that runs along the back of the house. If the big sliding walls of the bedrooms are open you can see straight through the house and out to Lake Wakatipu. "Wow" is a word that sprung childishly to mind as I slumped down in a broad expanse of armchair in the sitting area. The lake seems to stretch out from beneath the house itself, seen through huge slabs of glass that jut triangularly like a ship's prow. No one could say that Twin Peaks does not make the most of its view. On the other side of the lake rise the Remarkables, a range of skiing mountains with those two peaks after which the house is named. Outside is a barbecue area and bedrooms have an oriental openness to the design, clean marble in the bathrooms and all-glass showers. And while the house itself might be cool and minimalist, leaving you unsure if you are inside or outside, Margaret and Derek are contrastingly warm, direct and friendly people who have clearly loved meeting all their guests. You are offered early evening drinks with them, a good time to sort out all that there is to do in Queenstown. *Biking and walking track to Queenstown, jet-boating, white-water rafting, parapenting, skiing, flights to Milford Sound.*

Rooms: 2: both queens with en/s showers.
Price: $340.
Meals: Full breakfast included. About 130 restaurants in Queenstown.
Directions: From Frankton village go 2.4km in the Queenstown direction on State Highway 6A. Twin Peaks is on your left. There is no large B&B sign. Look for number 661 on the letterbox and go to the end of the driveway.

Tranquillity Lodge

Margaret and Peter Gibson
76 Wesney Terrace, Kingston
Tel: 03-248-8819 Fax: 03-248-8819
Email: info@tranquillitylodge.co.nz Web: www.tranquillitylodge.co.nz
Cell: 0274-336-829

South Islanders Margaret and Peter have known about Kingston's gems for 40 years. This quiet Lake Wakatipu backwater is home to 200 residents, the iconic Kingston Flyer steam train, a nine-hole golf course, beautiful nature walks, a fun little tavern serving simple, tasty, rural tucker (I recommend the seafood chowder) and just a very relaxed air that settles over you and calms you down. The view may have had something to do with it. Tranquillity Lodge has floor-to-ceiling windows in the sitting room that open onto the deck and the front lawn. This in turn glides down to the glassy lake's shingle beach and some uninhibited views of the Hector Range, the Remarkables, Eyre Mountain and Coronet Peak on the distant horizon. Peter has all the gear that you need to make the most of your stay: fishing rods, kayaks, mountain-bikes, golf clubs. Or there are nice deck chairs under the lakefront willow tree, if you're more of a reader. The lodge is comfortable with a private kitchen and sitting room with flat-screen TV and DVDs. The suites are not huge, but thoughtfully welcoming with the Pinot room being the pick of the two simply for its brilliant view. So yes, it's relaxed here. This is holidaying New Zealand style, in a quiet nature-blessed setting away from the bright lights. If you want something hassle-free, something memorable, then Kingston's the place and the warm-hearted Gibsons are the people.

Rooms: 2: 1 queen and 1 superking/twin.
Price: $200 - $225.
Meals: Full breakfast included. Peter can whip up an evening platter by arrangement which includes a complimentary bottle of New Zealand wine.
Directions: Heading south on SH6, turn into the main street of Kingston (Kent St), then turn right into Churchill St to the lake front. Take the road to the right and it's the last house on the waterfront.

Pencarrow

Bill and Kari Moers

678 Frankton Road, Queenstown
Tel: 03-442-8938 Fax: 03-442-8974
Email: info@pencarrow.net Web: www.pencarrow.net
Cell: 027-413-1567

Bill and Kari used to enjoy the high life, literally, working as crew on a Saudi prince's private jet. Old habits die hard, though, and they're still high, on a beautiful hillside property on the edge of Queenstown. Best place to admire the view is probably from one of the window-seats in a hugely relaxing guest lounge, toes warmed by the fire in winter, spirits soothed by one of the hordes of CDs. Once you've revived, there's croquet and horseshoes outside; or a games room with a dartboard, a beautiful 19th-century billiard table and some eye-catching paraphernalia proudly displayed – each piece has a story. There are four luxurious suites with separate sitting-rooms, sleigh beds, chunky sofas, balconies, double sinks, entertainment systems – the list of positives is a veritable Mississippi. A Dallas designer with an eye for colour gave the rooms their character. The views are special from all the suites. Bill and Kari, charming Americans both, are so generous and relaxed you'll feel like you're staying with long-lost relatives. They even insist on offering breakfast (Bill's 'eggs on a cloud' are not to be missed) whenever their guests want and will even serve you in bed, if floor-to-ceiling windows in the dining-room can't tempt you. One last thing... the loo by the entrance hall, created by Kari's mother, is one of the finest I've seen.

Rooms: 4 suites: 3 superkings and 1 king; all with en-suite spa and shower and all with sitting-rooms. 2 have extra sofa beds
Price: $595. Plus $95 for an extra person.
Meals: Full breakfast included.
Directions: From the east, enter Queenstown on Frankton Rd. Pass Shell Garage on your right. 1.2km further, turn right at Greenstone Terrace and Remarkables Apartments and you'll see the drive up to Pencarrow (No. 678). Approx 4km from Queenstown.

Mountain Range

Owners Stuart and Melanie Pinfold; Managers Chris Shaw and Erica Wymore
Heritage Park, Cardrona Valley Rd, Wanaka
Tel: 03-443-7400 Fax: 03-443-7450
Email: stay@mountainrange.co.nz Web: www.mountainrange.co.nz

I chatted with Erica and Chris over freshly-ground coffee and Erica's hot-that-very-morning home-baking. The day was gorgeous and I just soaked up the sun and the company of this young and very engaging couple. They started out in New Zealand as travellers, working their way around the country and eventually settling down at Mountain Range. It's a dreamy environment they have here - a large weatherboard and schist stone lodge built on a quiet parkland plot, surrounded by grass, two minutes outside Wanaka. The lodge was designed to make the most of the light and does so admirably. A homely sitting-room lures you in with its large fire, comfy sofas, Sky TV, DVD collection and book exchange. I could not resist this warm heart of the house for a minute, not even to slip outside and into the new Canadian-style hot tub in the garden - more fool me. And finally to sleep, in a spotless, understated bedroom with its supreme bed and vibrant NZ artworks, its spa in the en-suite bathroom (all bathrooms have heated floors) and its views over frosty lawns to distant mountains. Those mountain views - of the Aspiring, Crown and Criffel ranges - pop up on all sides of the lodge, which is terribly handy for those who like their soul-sharpening moments easily accessible. *Hiking, fishing, biking, golf and excellent skiing.*

Rooms: 7 superkings/twins; 1 with en-suite spa and shower, 6 with en-suite shower.
Price: $220 - $340.
Meals: Full breakfast included. Complimentary afternoon tea and a glass of local wine to enjoy at your leisure.
Directions: From Queenstown via Cardrona: lodge is on R after Café Fe, just before Wanaka. From Wanaka: follow signs to Cardrona, turning up McDougall St, and Heritage Park is next L after Golf Course Rd. Lodge is first drive on L.

Lime Tree Lodge

Rebecca Butts and Sally Carwardine
672 Ballantyne Road, Wanaka
Tel: 03-443-7305 Fax: 03-443-7345
Email: revive@limetreelodge.co.nz Web: www.limetreelodge.co.nz
Cell: 021-529-118

No matter which way you look from Lime Tree Lodge's manicured garden, some distant, grandly-named mountain will stare right back at you. The lodge, humbled and alone among its rocky neighbours, is uniquely positioned on a huge, flat plain, so that with a single quick and dizzy spin you can view them all at once. Although just a quick drive away, I felt perfectly removed from the bustle of town as I pondered the panorama, not quite knowing where to rest my eyes – so I stepped inside and set my sights on some well-needed R&R instead. Dominated by a superb, craggy schist fireplace the living area is stylish-yet-put-your-feet-up-and-sink-into-the-sofa-right-now comfy all at the same time. Though new to the business, your hosts Sally and Rebecca seem instinctively to know just what you'll need. For me this meant cracking open a bottle of local pinot noir, preparing a delicious tray of nibbles, including Rebecca's whitebait 'fritters' fresh from the pan, and stoking the fire till it crackled. Perfect. All the rooms are fresh and contemporary, but just as cosy. Plenty of light streams through their French windows from Rebecca's lovely garden, which is just the spot to relax and soak up the warm Central Otago sun. Enjoy a Vodka lime gimlet - Lime Tree Lodge's suggested apéritif made with New Zealand's very own '42 below' Vodka and freshly-squeezed lime juice – with your hosts while the sun sets over awe-inspiring mountains in the distance. *Swimming-pool, petanque court, 5-hole pitch, putt golf course on site. Kids over 8 welcome.*

Rooms: 6: 2 superking/twin, 2 king/twin, all en/s sh'r; 2 superior suites (lounge, sat TV, CD/DVD player, bar/fridge), 1 with log fire, kitchenette, dining area. Black Peak Suite: 1 superking/tw & 1 tw/bunk sharing en/s bath & sh'r (max 2 adults & 2 kids 12 & under); Linden Suite: 1 superking/tw en/s sh'r.
Price: $395 - $695. Transfers to & from Wanaka airport & into Wanaka (6 - 8 pm) also included.
Meals: Full breakfast incl'. Complimentary apéritifs, all day tea, coffee, home-baking, fruit, mineral water. Evening meals by prior arrangement in winter only.
Directions: Leave Wanaka on SH6 towards Queenstown. Lodge signed on R 6km from town. 7 mins from Wanaka.

Map Number: 5

Entry Number: 74

The Stone Cottage

Belinda Wilson

Dublin Bay Rd, Wanaka
Tel: 03-443-1878 Fax: 03-443-1276
Email: stonecottage@xtra.co.nz Web: www.stonecottage.co.nz

Belinda looks after her guests with a quiet, friendly competence. Dublin Bay is where her family had a holiday home and now she has returned. The Stone Cottage is her home and that of Brandy her dog, while the floor above houses an apartment and a smaller studio where guests stay. You are fully self-contained up there with kitchen(-ette), breakfast matériel provided in the fridge each morning (croissants, cereals, jams, fresh fruit, lots of teas), Sky TV, music, magazines. The smaller of the two has its own wooden deck and chairs while you can see the lake from bed in the other. The house is secluded and surrounded by a spectacular spring and autumn garden. It was hiding coyly under a frosty May rime when I was there, but the prognosis was excellent! A four-minute stroll will take you down to Lake Wanaka, ideal for swimming with its sandy beach and framed, as always in New Zealand, by a background of mountains. When not chilling out in the garden or fishing on the lake, many of Belinda's guests are doing the outdoorsy activities for which Wanaka is increasingly famed… including skiing. Belinda is there if you want her very relaxed company.

Rooms: 2 apartments; 1 sleeps 4 (queen and twin beds, bath/shower); the other has a superking and en-suite shower.
Price: $260 - $290. $40 per extra person.
Meals: Full breakfast provisions provided for you to cook your own. Dinners by prior arrangement $55 - $70.
Directions: From Wanaka take State Highway 6 for about 1.5km. Turn left where signed to Lake Hawea/West Coast. Follow over the bridge up the hill, turn left where signed to Dublin Bay Rd. Follow signs to house for 3km.

South Island - Otago

Entry Number: 75

Map Number: 5

Maple Lodge

Bernadette and Paul Raymont

56 Halliday Road, Wanaka
Tel: 03-443-6275 Fax: 03-443-6274
Email: stay@maplelodgewanaka.co.nz Web: www.maplelodgewanaka.co.nz

Wanaka is a destination for all seasons and Maple Lodge has been thoughtfully designed to cater for them all. I sat at the dining table on a hot summer afternoon, a soft breeze fanning through the big open doors, and I revived myself with steady sips of ice water while I contemplated my surroundings. The lounge would be an ideal place to hibernate away on winter evenings. I could imagine dumping my ski gear in the drying room and repairing to the schist log-burner, with its leather sofas, rugs and the odd conversation piece mounted on the walls (such as the pitchfork grown from a single piece of wood). The courtyard and gardens suit spring and autumn, great spots from which to appreciate the fiery turning of the maple trees, as free-range chickens scurry through the new grass, before easing into the outdoor hot tub, or playing 'Lord of the Rings', an eye-catching game invented by Bernadette and built from Dunedin wharf's recycled foundations. The view, though, is a year-round marvel: Mt Gold, Mt Maud, Mt Iron and the distant Black Peak. You can see some of these from the bedrooms, each of which has been individually decorated by Bernadette. All the rooms are very comfortable, with custom-made New Zealand furniture, personally-collected wall art and plenty of extras. So whether you're here to ski during winter or trek in spring, swim in summer or wine-taste in autumn, you can't go wrong at Maple Lodge.

Rooms: 7: 5 kings and 2 superking/twins, all with en/s showers.
Price: $250 - $335. Check web site for special rates.
Meals: Full breakfast, evening apéritif & afternoon tea incl. Free lift to recommended restaurants. Packed lunches and evening meals provided by prior arrangement.
Directions: Maple Lodge is about 3 minutes' drive from Wanaka. Head out of the main town on SH84, past Puzzle World into SH6, then take a left into Halliday Road, Maple Lodge is on your right.

Map Number: 5

Silverpine

Susan and Mike Yates

The Neck, Wanaka
Tel: 03-443-9008 Fax: 03-443-4234
Email: info@silverpine.co.nz Web: www.silverpine.co.nz

Brooding from its rocky vantage, Silverpine is positioned on a bluff that bridges the beautiful Lakes Wanaka and Hawea. It is the only building for miles and its setting, amid the snow-peaked Southern Alps, is not a breath away from extraordinary. I decided to trek to the lodge through waist-high grass, stopping every now and then to gaze out on a pastoral idyll of dusky mountains and glassy lakes and to watch the falcons wheeling high above a herd of deer. When I finally made it to Silverpine, as night was falling, I waited for appropriate words to reach my lips and just settled on 'wow'. The lodge is beautifully designed to blend and not compete with its surroundings. From the sheep-skin strewn, pebbled (and heated!) long window-seats in the elegantly neutral bedrooms to the giant silverpine beams in the high ceilings, the magnificent 14-foot black pine dining table and the slabs of rock that cover the floors, everything here is natural, earthy and strong. Mike has carved most of the furniture himself from timber collected over the years from the West Coast, and with each piece there is a tale to be told. Fittingly, Sue, who originally comes from Hawaii and Mike, a sub-Antarctic fisherman in a former life, are two of the most genuinely down-to-earth and interesting people I met in NZ. Special mention for Sue's superb cooking... her scallops on saffron risotto are an absolute sensation. But then trust me, everything about this place is great, almost perfectly so. *Helicopter rides available.*

Rooms: 4: all superking/twin with en-suite deep bath and shower.
Price: $750. Singles $600. Price includes 3-course dinner.
Meals: Full breakfast. Dinner included in price. Wine list available.
Directions: From Wanaka take SH6 for approx 38km towards the Haast Pass and West Coast. Just before The Neck of Lake Hawea, Silverpine is the only building high up on the left. From the Makarora/Haast/West Coast side, the lodge is 1.8km from The Neck on the right and Lake Hawea will be on your left.

Murrell's Grand View House

Robert and Philippa Murrell

7 Murrell Avenue, Manapouri
Tel: 03-249-6642 Fax: 03-249-6966
Email: murrell@xtra.co.nz Web: www.murrells.co.nz

Any visitor to Murrell's who arrives in daylight will be instantly drawn, as I was, to the incredible view from the garden of Lake Manapouri, surely one of the most beautiful bodies of water in the world. You can walk down via woods to the lakeside or set off along birdsong-supported tracks of the Fiordland National Park. The Waiau River is where you take the boats out to Doubtful Sound, a fantastic day out. Both the river and the lake are only a 5 minute walk away. If it rains, all the cliff waterfalls erupt with water and cascade into the sea ... and if it's fine, well, then it's fine. Dolphins are often seen, seals always. But Rob can tell you all about it. He was born here, grew up here, worked these skies as a pilot, the rivers as a jet-boat driver and the roads as a coachman. He knows Southland well and so did his ancestors who were among the first to settle here and conquer many of the local peaks. Amazingly the house was built 120 years ago by Rob's great-grandfather. Today it's run by fourth-generation Rob, his wife Philippa and their two children Zoë (10) and Will (7) who occasionally pitch in. The house retains the original simplicity of a historic homestead of this type, with old fittings and the aged family boar and stag trophies in the hallway. The bedrooms are spacious and light-filled, with good beds and good-quality linen. Group dinners can be arranged and they're a fun affair, especially with Philippa and Rob, two very likable people, playing host. Murrell's is a very characterful place to base yourself when visiting Doubtful Sound and the Fiordland National Park.

Rooms: 4: king, superking/twin, 1 queen, 1 queen/twin/triple. All with en/s shower.
Price: 1 person: $300; 2 people: $325; 3 people: $420.
Meals: Full breakfast included. Complimentary refreshment and fresh baking on arrival. Dinners at additional cost and by prior arrangment.
Directions: Follow SH95 into Manapouri, which becomes Waiau Street. Keep going until the shop and the petrol station. Murrell's is opposite, behind the Macrocarpa Hedge with the red roof.

Map Number: 6

Fiordland Lodge

Robynne and Ron Peacock

472 Te Anau - Milford Highway, Te Anau
Tel: 03-249-7832 Fax: 03-249-7449
Email: info@fiordlandlodge.co.nz Web: www.fiordlandlodge.co.nz

That's quite some window they've got there. You're out in the country 5km from Te Anau, near a lake, near the mountains. Any window stands a good chance of impressing. But this one? Wow. Entering Fiordland Lodge you're assaulted by a wall of glass rising some 30 feet, through which you look westwards across the grassland to Lake Te Anau and the forested lower slopes of Mt Luxmore. The large sitting area that confronts this view has deep armchairs and sofas, with a bar in the corner in case it all gets too much. In the middle of the room vast supporting trunks of silver beech compete for attention with a river stone fireplace that uses old bridge beams from the Milford Road. Everything in this building, built in 2002, is natural. Smart bedrooms use earth colours, chunky beams and relaxing spot lighting. Bathrooms are particularly handsome, with basins on wooden benches, more natural tones and big wicker baskets. And sumptuous dinners - included in the lodge prices - are served in the dining-room, which also looks west. Away from the lodge there are many natural activities - Ron was a National Park ranger and guides fishermen, bird-watchers and nature lovers in the Fiordland National Park. There are also two cheaper chalets, where dinner in the lodge is an optional extra.

Rooms: 10 rooms in lodge: 9 lodge rooms, all kings/twins, all with en-suite showers; 1 Executive Suite, with king/twin, 1 ensuite spa/shower; 2 log cabins, with queen bed and 3 singles, 2 with en-suite spa/shower.
Price: Room rates are for two people, including dinner and breakfast. Lodge rooms $580 (winter) - $900 (summer); Executive Suite $680 (winter) - $1,100 (summer); log cabins $480 (winter) - $680 (summer). Extra adult $220, child $180 - $200.
Meals: Full breakfast and 4-course dinner, table d'hôte, included for all.
Directions: Follow signs to Milford Sound out of Te Anau. After nearly 5km Fiordland Lodge signed to R.

Nokomai Station

Brian and Ann Hore

SH 6 (Queenstown - Te Anau Highway)
Tel: 03-248-8850 and 03-248-8837 Fax: 03-248-8841
Email: nokomai@xtra.co.nz Web: www.nokomai.co.nz
Cell: 027-242-9480

Far, far from the madding crowd, on an astonishing 100,000 acres of Southland farmland you find Nokomai. One of the largest privately-owned stations in the country, it's home to 50,000 sheep, 2,000 cattle, horses and dogs as well as the station's staff and families. The location is a ruralist's dream and the driveway no less so. Leaving the Queenstown road, you criss-cross the Mataura River three times before turning along the banks of Nokomai Creek and onwards to the farm, which sits at the end of a light-filled valley. Accommodation is in four comfortable, purpose-built cottages where you can either self-cater or have your meals provided. There is plenty to do here; it is not a place to arrive at 6 and leave at 8 the next morning. You can watch the seasonal farm activities, walk forever, borrow mountain bikes, fish for trout with guides on the famous Mataura River (20km of which runs through the property), or you can even try your hand at 'golfcross' - trust a bunch of Kiwis to invent a form of golf that's played with a rugby-shaped golf ball and posts! Or, more glamorously, you can go 'flightseeing' with Nokomai helicopters. You can hire man and machine to go just about anywhere, from a tour of the station to Milford Sound, and do almost any activity: he'll even drop you on a mountain top at sunset with a bottle of champagne.

Rooms: 4 self-catering cottages: 2 with 1 king/twin, 2 with 2 kings/twins in different rooms.
Price: $250 for one bedroom cottage. $320 for 2 bedroom cottage. $380 for the newly-built cottage.
Meals: Full breakfast included. $15 pp for packed lunch. Dinner $65 pp (includes beer and wine).
Directions: From Queenstown, head towards Te Anau on Hwy 6. Turn left 5km south of Athol onto Nokomai Road. Go 12km to the station.

Sails Ashore

Iris and Peter Tait

11 View Street, Stewart Islan
Tel: Freephone 0800-783-9278 or 03-219-1151 Fax: 03-219-1151
Email: tait@sailsashore.co.nz Web: www.sailsashore.co.nz

You'll struggle and then fail to find anyone who knows Stewart Island better than the interesting, intelligent, warm-hearted Taits, who have lived here for 40 years and whose southern hospitality is so genuine and natural. Peter's tours are enthusiastic, entertaining and his knowledge of the island's history, birdlife, plants, walking tracks and coast is unmatched, particularly on Ulva Island, a pristine, predator-free sanctuary for rare and endangered bird and plant species. Sails Ashore's chic suites - skillfully-created rope chairs (I want one), fine linen, fridge, tea/coffee, surround-sound DVD and Iris's home baking - are built with salvaged rimu and if there's a theme it is nature. All these factors combine to make each room your own homely space. There's no expense spared. Peter's even designed a heated closet rack to dry out your hiking boots. The guest lounge is a treasure house of curiosities, such as the sea chest from Peter's grandfather's ship-jumping days, but there's a story behind every object. Despite an extensive library, reading may be difficult with one eye constantly drawn outside to the constantly-changing mood and weather over Halfmoon Bay. It can be mesmerising, unless you're distracted by the cheeky, inquisitive kakas who hop and groove across the deck outside. It is isolated here, but it's definitely worth the effort. Stewart Island is incomparable and officially one of my most recommended New Zealand treasures for reviving the spirit… and that goes for Sails Ashore too.

Rooms: 2: both king/twin with en/s shower.
Price: $420. 2 night minimum stay. Guided walks: $95 for guests.Road tours: $45 for guests.
Meals: Complimentary continental breakfast with fresh croissants, fruit, baking, frozen yoghurt, mueslis, good coffee and Iris's rhubarb.
Directions: Arrange booking with Iris and Peter, then fly or ferry to Stewart Island, let the Taits know your time of arrival and they'll pick you up. The house is close to the main restaurants and town.

Mahitahi Lodge

John Birchfield and Jacqui Low
State Highway 6, Bruce Bay
Tel: 03-751-0095 Fax: 03-751-0195
Email: stay@mahitahilodge.co.nz Web: www.mahitahilodge.co.nz
Cell: Freephone in NZ 0800-751-009

Night was falling when I finally drove into Bruce Bay - and out the other side again. Quite a feat when you consider that there are only three permanent dwellings in this tiny West Coast settlement. Once the site of a thriving road-building town (in the thirties the village hall hosted black-tie balls complete with swing orchestra), Bruce Bay is now a close-knit rural community. Within five minutes of my locating Mahitahi, I was safely ensconced in front of the roaring fire, chatting away with a glass of pinot noir in hand. Jacqui is an accountant by trade, while John, a self-professed "hunter-gatherer" has a background in forestry and fishing. His fingers are the deepest shade of green, so naturally the jade-coloured broccoli and iron-rich new potatoes at supper were home-grown. Ask him to take you on a tour of the area and you'll find out about the growth cycle of the kahikatea tree, local Maori history and how to pan for gold - he has his very own concession. The couple built the house themselves from salvaged indigenous wood. Upstairs is a soaring loft space drenched in natural light, with wooden beams, rose-brown rimu furniture and walls painted the colour of bark. The forest theme continues into the bedrooms. I stayed in 'Rimu' a cosy affair with a russet-maroon bedspread and chocolates on the bed. The bathrooms have under-floor heating as well, perfect for drying off soggy boots after a long day's tramping.

Rooms: 3: Rimu Room and Totara Room both super-king or twin rooms with en/s shower; Matai Family Room with queen bed, shower, adjoining kitchenette and lounge with sofa bed.
Price: $325 inc. breakfast.
Meals: Cooked breakfast included: eggs, bacon, porridge, plus cereals, fresh yoghurt and jams. Evening meals, $70 inc. wine.
Directions: Thirty miles south of the Fox Glacier on State Highway 6. On your left-hand side as you drive through Bruce Bay.

Holly Homestead B&B

Gerard and Bernie Oudemans
2900 Franz Josef Highway, Franz Josef Glacier
Tel: 03-752-0299 Fax: 03-752-0298
Email: stay@hollyhomestead.co.nz Web: www.hollyhomestead.co.nz

Gerard and Bernie had just completed breakfast when the Greenwood Guides first barged into their lives having heard good things about them in town. It was an immediately comforting scene: wooden table, pieces of toast in racks, the smell of real coffee and freshly-baked bread. This 1926 former farmhouse has been stripped back to its wooden heart: weatherboarded walls, polished floors, panelled ceilings, wooden windows. But the Oudemans continually improve it - with a spacious new kitchen area allowing for plenty of elbow room at the breakfast table, and most recently a delightful new suite. All rooms have comfortable beds and percale sheets, while upstairs there's a tiny balcony with wisteria and jasmine on one side and a roof terrace (facing the mountains and the sunset) on the other. Gerard and Bernie, both New Zealanders, have been in the B&B business since 2000 and are rightly enthusiastic about their magnificent region. They are still unstuffy and refreshingly modest about what they offer, although "we're getting better at blowing our own trumpet." And so they should, if only for the spectacular views from breakfast table, "clouds permitting!" Bernie adds. So self-deprecating you know you're going to like it. *Good base for Okarito, Franz Josef and Fox Glacier explorations. Scenic flights, guided glacier hikes, kayaking, horse-trekking, white heron sanctuary tour, kiwi tours at night. Children 12+ welcome.*

Rooms: 5: 2 superkings/twins, 1 superking, 2 queen; 3 with en-suite shower and 2 with en-suite bath and shower. Sitting-room for guests.
Price: $200 - $400. Check website for minimum night requirements and seasonal rates.
Meals: Full cooked breakfast included. There are plenty of restaurants in town for lunch and evening meals.
Directions: On main road 1.5km north from the Franz Josef village centre. 2900 Franz Josef Highway.

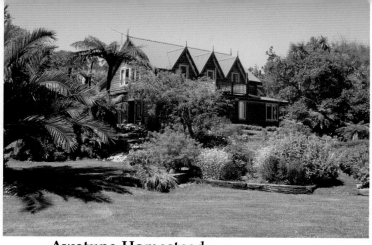

Awatuna Homestead

Pauline and Hêmi Te Rakau
9 Stafford Road, Awatuna, RD 2, Hokitika
Tel: 03-755-6834 Fax: 03-755-6876
Email: rest@awatunahomestead.co.nz Web: www.awatunahomestead.co.nz

A very laid-back, very happy home. If I were a bit older, I'd probably write about the 'vibe'. Here in the unspoilt coastal bush near Hokitika, Hêmi and Pauline's B&B manages to get everything right. Take the opportunity to relax by the open fire in the guest lounge accompanied by Maori-speaking Hêmi's intricate knowledge of local history and traditional Maori story-telling. Throw a fine wine list, Pauline's tempting cooking (using home-grown produce) into the mix and you won't find many that venture out at night in search of restaurants. The three handsome guest rooms are beautifully decorated in various colour schemes, with furniture picked up by Pauline from, oh, all over the place. The Goldsborough is the grandest with its elegant decor and double spa bath. And there is also a self-catering apartment. Outside are six acres of gardens and farmland with plenty of natives majestically thriving - just have a look at the kauri trees. A secluded spa pool (under cover for rainy days) is nestled away, where you can sit and gaze at the Milky Way. Accompanied by the bird life you can fish on the nearby beach or take a short walk to a look-out point in the bush. Poppy "the pop-up" dog, one proud cat, two horses, sheep and fresh-egg producing chooks are all in residence. Hêmi also restores Morris Eights; if you're well behaved, like I was, you might get a spin in one, like I did. So be good, because it's well worth it and I have to say, this is as much a promise to return as a write-up.

Rooms: 4: 1 self-contained apartment with 1 queen room and 1 twin room sharing bathroom (bath/shower); 1 superking/twin with en/s spa bath & shower; 1 superking/twin with en/s shower; 1 queen en/s shower. Guest lounge. Wireless email/fax facility.
Price: $280 - $360. Singles $30 less than the doubles.
Meals: Dinners $70 pp by prior arrangement, wine (list available) not included. Full breakfast served in the homestead included. In the apartment $25 pp.
Directions: From Greymouth follow signs to Hokitika. At Awatuna turn left into Stafford Road, signposted, and over the train tracks. Homestead is on the left.

Map Number: 7

Entry Number: 84

Rimu Lodge

Helen and Peter Walls

33 Seddon Terrace Road, Rimu, Hokitika
Tel: 03-755-5255 Fax: 03-755-5237
Email: rimulodge@xtra.co.nz Web: www.rimulodge.co.nz

Disa, the Walls' effervescent springer spaniel, frantically wagged me a welcome and led me to the door where I met Helen. She invited me into her purpose-built modern retreat and we wandered into the hallway where an array of eye-catching photography lines the wall, depicting local wildlife and scenery; Helen likes to exhibit local artists here, so it might be a good opportunity to purchase a favourite by which to remember your New Zealand adventure. You'll have plenty of time to consider your options over a complimentary wine on the broad outdoor deck, or beside the lounge's grand open fire built from smooth river rocks. The sandstone and clay-shaded room interiors are designed by Helen and she's done a great job with all the luxuries. They're named after some of New Zealand's famous avian beauties: Kereru, Tui, Korimako and Kotuku. While appreciating the views from each room, I struggled to picture this idyllic landscape blighted by mills and mines as it once was: now native birds flit around the tree tops of regenerating native bush, dairy cows meander to their distant milking shed and the stunning blue of the Hokitika River trims the edge of the Southern Alps. I wish I'd had time to kayak its surreally turquoise currents. I'll just have to come back, perhaps to try a spot of fishing along the deserted beach where baby seals rest during winter. They like this secluded coast… I expect you will too. *Broadband internet available.*

Rooms: 4: I superking/twin with en/s shower, I king with en/s shower, 2 queens with en/s shower.
Price: $295 - $365.
Meals: Full breakfast included.
Directions: On SH6 just south of Hokitika Bdge take Arthurstown Rd turn & go 4km to intersection (Kaniere Bdge), then R along Woodstock-Rimu Rd 3km. L onto Seddons Terrace Rd at Rimu. Lodge 300m on L. From south 11km north of Ross, R into Woodstock-Rimu Rd signed Rimu. Rimu 8km from turn. R into Seddons Terrace Rd.

Bird's Ferry Lodge and Ferryman's Cottage

Alison and André Gygax

Bird's Ferry Road, Charleston
Tel: 0800-212-207
Email: info@birdsferrylodge.co.nz Web: www.birdsferrylodge.co.nz
Cell: 021-337-217

Only five years old, a mere fledgling, yet Bird's Ferry Lodge seems nonetheless to have seamlessly nested upon its hilltop where it sits content, quietly musing on the far-reaching, sea-lined views. As I chatted with Alison and André from a snug sofa I tried to keep my attention on Greenwood Guides and away from the cinema-screen-sized window that frames the whole dramatic scene. Merlot and Mick, two whiskered, smiling, people-loving terriers, won me over at once, while the warming presence of an Aga in the kitchen (as rare as a traffic jam in New Zealand) reminded me of home. For Alison, a Celtic catering manager who just loves to cook, it was a must-have. Here foody treats are conjured from home-grown produce and resident chooks lay your eggs for breakfast. Originally from Cape Town, André has lived in New Zealand for the last 23 years and, with a past career as a guide, his knowledge of the country far exceeds that of any local. He's also a fully-qualified masseur and there's a massage room on site, if you should feel the need for even further relaxation. Also a very popular spa bath. At the end of the road, in twelve acres of seclusion, is the new cottage, with quirky driftwood furniture made by André, and disturbed only by kiwi calls at night. An old-fashioned bath sits out at the front, plumbed in with hot running water and perched over views stretching from sea to snow-covered mountain, just awaiting the glories of a sunset with a glass of bubbly in hand. Here there is no TV, no landline and no clock… just a wealth of peace, seclusion and beauty.

Rooms: 3: 2 queens with e/s bath/shower; 1 twin with en/s shower. All rooms have private deck & access. Self-catering cottage: 4-poster queen plus 1 superking room (twin/double), + sleep sofa in lounge; sleeps max 6.
Price: $200 - $350. Lodge stays of more that 2 nights include half a day's guiding with André. Cottage tariff $249 - $350 includes breakfast hamper.
Meals: Full breakfast incl' for lodge. Dinners by prior arrangement only: 3-course dinner (local produce): $80. Half bottle wine incl'. 2-course cottage dinner: $45.
Directions: 17km south of Westport, 8km north of Charleston on SH6. Signed on L coming from Charleston (R from Westport). Turn at sign & go 1.7km along private gravel road. Lodge at end of rd.

Map Number: 7

INDEX

Index By House Name

INDEX

Index By Nearest Town Name

INDEX OF ACTIVITIES

Gardens
Places with lovely gardens and owners who are enthusiastic gardeners.
5, 6, 7, 10, 13, 14, 20, 21, 22, 23, 26, 27, 28, 29, 30, 31, 32, 33, 34, 36, 38, 39, 41, 43, 45, 47, 48, 50, 51, 52, 54, 55, 57, 58, 60, 61, 62, 63, 64, 65, 66, 68, 72, 74, 75, 76, 78, 80, 81, 84, 85, 86

Rock art
Sites found either on the property or guests can be shown/guided to nearby sites.
13, 34

Culture
Cultural visits can be organized by owners.
2, 6, 8, 10, 11, 14, 19, 20, 30, 32, 33, 34, 36, 39, 40, 51, 52, 63, 64, 74, 80, 81, 82, 84,

Wine-maker
Wine made on the property.
50, 54, 61

Good and original cuisine
20, 21, 27, 31, 32, 34, 36, 38, 39, 41, 42, 44, 50, 52, 54, 60, 64, 65, 74, 77, 79, 80, 82, 86

Horse-riding
Available on site.
15, 27, 30, 32, 34, 37, 39, 40, 41, 44, 46, 51, 56, 58, 68, 74

Whale-watching
Available from the property or from so nearby that it makes little difference.
8, 9, 43, 53, 54, 58

Boat Charter
Property owns boats or can organise charters.
1, 2, 3, 5, 6, 8, 9, 10, 11, 12, 14, 16, 22, 23, 24, 25, 26, 27, 30, 31, 32, 34, 36, 37, 42, 43, 44, 45, 46, 47, 48, 49, 50, 51, 52, 53, 54, 57, 64, 68, 71, 74, 76, 77, 78, 81, 82

Canoeing
Canoes owned or organised by the property.
2, 3, 5, 6, 8, 9, 10, 11, 14, 15, 16, 23, 24, 25, 26, 30, 31, 32, 34, 36, 37, 38, 39, 40, 41, 42, 43, 44, 45, 46, 47, 48, 50, 51, 52, 53, 54, 55, 57, 58, 64, 71, 74, 76, 78, 81, 82, 86

Historic house
These places are historic buildings
19, 29, 33, 40, 41, 47, 48, 49, 56, 62, 63, 65, 66, 68, 78, 80, 84

History tours
Organised here
8, 19, 20, 32, 33, 37, 40, 41, 52, 68, 74, 82

Self-catering option available here
1, 2, 3, 4, 5, 8, 11, 12, 14, 15, 16, 19, 21, 22, 26, 28, 30, 31, 33, 35, 37, 39, 40, 41, 42, 43, 44, 45, 46, 48, 50, 52, 53, 54, 56, 58, 59, 75, 80, 82, 84, 86

Bird-watching
Owners are enthusiasts.
1, 5, 8, 9, 15, 16, 21, 23, 26, 27, 30, 32, 33, 34, 37, 38, 39, 40, 41, 43, 44, 45, 46, 47, 50, 51, 52, 53, 54, 55, 56, 60, 61, 64, 65, 68, 71, 78, 79, 80, 81, 82, 84, 85, 86

Beach house
1, 2, 3, 12, 14, 16, 23, 24, 25, 43, 53

White-water rafting
Can be arranged in-house.
32, 34, 36, 39, 40, 41, 54, 58, 64, 74, 76

Fully child-friendly
Places where children will be particularly well looked-after.
8, 14, 15, 16, 19, 22, 26, 34, 41, 48, 61, 62, 65, 66, 84,

THE GREENWOOD GUIDE TO
SOUTH AFRICA
hand-picked accommodation

Now in 8th edition. Annual editions published in June each year.

This guide-book contains some 350 B&Bs, guest houses, game lodges, self-catering places and farms. Each place has been personally visited by the authors and chosen for its great charm, character and friendliness.

This book is designed for holiday-makers, both Southern African and from overseas, who want to travel independently, avoid mass tourism and meet friendly, humorous and hospitable people at every turn.

With 10 years' research and 7 previous editions already under our belt, and rigorous annual updates ensuring the standard goes up year by year, this has now become the flagship GG title.

Order form

	copy(ies)	price (each)	subtotal
THE GREENWOOD GUIDE TO SOUTH AFRICA Hand-picked accommodation (LATEST EDITION)		£13.95	
THE GREENWOOD GUIDE TO NEW ZEALAND Hand-picked accommodation (LATEST EDITION)		£9.95	

post and packing costs
£2 per order in the UK, NZ or South Africa
£3 per order within Europe, £4 per order elsewhere   **Total**

Name

Address to send the book to

Payment is by UK sterling cheque made out to 'Greenwood Guides Ltd' or by VISA/Mastercard (only)

Card number

Expiry date

CCV number

Please send this coupon to: 12 Avalon Rd, Fulham, London, SW6 2EX, UK

The Greenwood Guides also cover Canada and Australia.
These guides are now online titles only.

www.greenwoodguides.com